CONFLICT RESOLUTION QUARTERLY

Editorial Board Members

Conflict Resolution Quarterly (ISSN 1536-5581) (formerly *Mediation Quarterly*) is published quarterly by Wiley Subscription Services, Inc., A Wiley Company, at Jossey-Bass and is sponsored by the Association for Conflict Resolution. A subscription is included as a benefit of membership. For information about becoming a member of the Association of Conflict Resolution, please contact ACR's membership department at (202) 667-9700, ext. 206, or via e-mail at membership@acresolution.org.

Conflict Resolution Quarterly (formerly *Mediation Quarterly*) is indexed in PsycINFO, Sociological Abstracts, the National Child Support Enforcement Clearinghouse, and the International Bibliography of the Social Sciences.

TO ORDER subscriptions or single issues, please refer to the Ordering Information page at the back of this issue.

EDITORIAL CORRESPONDENCE: see the Information for Contributors pages at the back of this issue.

Note: Mediation Quarterly *was numbered consecutively from 1 to 24 from its inception through the Summer 1989 issue. From Fall 1989 to Summer 2001,* Mediation Quarterly *was numbered by volume and issue, beginning with Vol. 7, No. 1. From Fall 2001,* Conflict Resolution Quarterly *is numbered by volume and issue beginning with Vol. 19, No. 1.*

www.josseybass.com

CONTENTS

EDITOR'S INTRODUCTION   133

ARTICLES

Peer Mediation Training and Program Implementation in
Elementary Schools: Research Results   137
Kathy Bickmore

An evaluation of the Center for Conflict Resolution's peer mediation program in twenty-eight Cleveland public schools adds more evidence about the value of these efforts for developing student conflict competence and improving learning environments. Unique aspects of the Cleveland program, including peer involvement in training and mentoring of other students, are analyzed with respect to implementation issues and advantages.

Structural Sources of Conflict in a University Context   161
Allan Edward Barsky

What are the structural factors that act as sources of conflict in universities? This qualitative study answers that question from the perspective of students, faculty members, administrators, and the non-teaching staff. The results are presented in light of the unique organizational characteristics of universities providing insight for practitioners of higher education workplace conflict resolution.

COLLOQUY: TALKING IN AND ABOUT CONFLICT—DISCOURSE STUDIES OF CONFLICT PROCESSES

What Mediators Do with Words: Implementing Three Models of
Rational Discussion in Dispute Mediation   177
Scott Jacobs, Mark Aakhus

How do mediators interpret conflict situations? This article suggests that mediators rely on three dominant interpretive frames—critical discussion, bargaining, and therapy—and how their frames influence the substance, direction, and outcome of mediation. Working from these three models of rational discourse, the authors suggest a theory of mediator competence, focusing on which model to implement and how to best implement any model discursively.

Disputing Neutrality: A Case Study of a Bias Complaint
During Mediation   205
Angela Cora Garcia, Kristie Vise, Stephen Paul Whitaker
Most mediators endorse a philosophy that they should behave in a nonbiased
manner toward disputants. This case study takes a careful look at how mediator behaviors, whether intended or not, can create the perception of
mediator bias. Specific examples of emotion work, summarization, and questioning behaviors reveal potential traps mediators can work to avoid.

Discourses in the Use and Emergence of Organizational Conflict   231
Iwona L. Kusztal
There has been little research on how organizational conflicts actually
emerge, develop, and change. Research addressing this question has usually
focused on personality and structural factors as sources of conflict. A better
understanding of these processes is invaluable for practitioners seeking to
effectively prevent and manage conflicts. This extensive study locates the
source of emerging conflicts in the different discourses used by organizational
members.

BOOK REVIEW

Review of Kestner and Ray's *The Conflict Resolution Training
Program: Leader's Manual.* San Francisco: Jossey-Bass, 2002.   249
Melinda Ostermeyer

READER RESPONSE

False Dichotomies and Asking the Right Questions:
Response to Chia and others' "Enacting and Reproducing Social
and Individual Identity Through Mediation," *Conflict Resolution
Quarterly,* 2000, *19* (1), 49–74.   253
John Wade

EDITOR'S INTRODUCTION

My introductory comments to this issue are going to be quite brief in order to guarantee ample space for the contributions of the authors sharing their ideas with you. But I did want to preview some upcoming developments for *Conflict Resolution Quarterly (CRQ)* as well as provide a basic introduction to this issue.

Let me begin with some very good news. *CRQ* has been added to Wiley InterScience, one of the world's leading providers of on-line scientific, technical, medical, and professional content. Wiley InterScience currently hosts over 350 journals with a usership of over six million people around the world. If you want more information, see the Website at www.interscience.wiley.com. Our scholarship will be reaching ever-increasing audiences with this move. Thank you, Jossey-Bass and Wiley.

Approximately one year ago, my Editor's Introduction for the inaugural issue of *CRQ* indicated that the journal was a work in progress and that we would be adding new features to further achieve the journal's mission of publishing scholarship on the relationship between theory, research, and practice in the conflict management and dispute resolution field, to promote more effective professional applications. I am pleased to announce that we will be adding a new feature, starting with volume 20 issue number 3: "Research Matters."

Research Matters* will contain a short description of contemporary research published throughout the field that has important implications for practice. About one thousand to two thousand words will be devoted to very brief abstracts of studies and a discussion of how this new information may prove valuable to the scholar-practitioners of the Association for Conflict Resolution. Each Research Matters section will focus on a particular area of work (for example, the latest research on environmental mediation). The research summarized in this new section can come from studies published in other journals, research reports to funders, or evaluation research reports. If you are interested in identifying work you believe should be included, please send your suggestions to me at tsjones@astro.temple.edu.

* Of course, the name for the feature was inspired by Cornel West's wonderful book title Race Matters.

In this issue, we continue with two features that we have added in volume 20 of *CRQ*. Melinda Ostermeyer continues the book review feature with her review of Kestner and Ray's *The Conflict Resolution Training Program: Leader's Manual*. And John Wade continues the Reader Response feature with his comments on Chia and others' article "Enacting and Reproducing Social and Individual Identity Through Mediation."

The colloquy in this issue concentrates on studies of discourse in conflict processes. Increasing our field has become more sensitive to the importance of discourse analysis in understanding how conflict is enacted as a social process. More micro-level analysis can yield important insights about practitioners' orientation, bias, and intervention. For managing conflict, discourse is our primary diagnostic, prevention, and intervention tool.

The three articles in the colloquy explore the power of discourse in mediation and organizational conflict.** Scott Jacobs and Mark Aakhus present three models of rationality revealed in mediators' discourse. Their analysis suggests that mediators orient to disputes from a bargaining frame, a therapeutic frame, or a critical discussion frame. The mediator's rationality is revealed in his or her discourse and influences disputants to use discourse that is consonant with the mediator's rationality. Jacobs and Aakhus remind us that subtle influence is nevertheless a powerful influence.

Angela Cora Garcia, Kristie Vise, and Stephen Paul Whitaker give us a fascinating example of how a mediator's discourse can lead to perceptions of bias among disputants. They were able to capture ongoing dialogue in a mediation in which one of the disputants made a claim of bias against the mediator. Garcia and her colleagues take us through the discourse to help us understand how the mediator's behavior (no matter how inadvertent) led to serious consequences. And, of course, their analysis yields very valuable practice information—what mediators probably want to avoid.

Iwona L. Kusztal reports on a yearlong qualitative study of one university administrative unit that explored how organizational conflicts emerge and are transformed through "discourses in use." She helps us see that organizational members understand conflicts in terms of various professional, political, and human relations, as well as in terms of discourses. And she helps us see that the source of many organizational conflicts lies in the use of different—and often competing—discourses.

** The authors in the colloquy used Gail Jefferson's discourse analysis notation system to present discourse examples. In the interest of space and readability, I made an editorial decision to simplify the presentation of the text in the examples. For the discourse analysts in our audience, please rest assured that these scholars used every care in their initial reporting of textual detail.

Our conventional articles in this issue are contributed by Kathy Bickmore and Allan Edward Barsky. Bickmore reports her evaluation of the Center for Conflict Resolution's peer mediation program in twenty-eight Cleveland public schools. Her work continues to inform us about best practices in conflict resolution education. Barsky answers the question What are the structural factors that act as sources of conflict in universities? The results are presented in light of the unique organizational characteristics of universities providing insight for practitioners of higher education workplace conflict resolution.

TRICIA S. JONES
Editor-in-Chief

Peer Mediation Training and Program Implementation in Elementary Schools: Research Results

KATHY BICKMORE

This research examines the implementation and effects of a peer mediation program in twenty-eight urban elementary schools. The Center for Conflict Resolution, a program of the Cleveland, Ohio, public schools, provided intensive training and follow-up support for teams of peer mediators and adult advisers at each school. Trainers were youths from the same community. Qualitative and quantitative evidence indicate that this program significantly improved the average eight- to eleven-year-old student's understanding of and inclination to use nonviolent conflict resolution and his or her capacity to achieve in school. The study outlines the specific commitments from administrators and other staff members that were required to develop and implement equitable, effective, and sustainable programs.

Until the last few years, little systematic research was available regarding the implementation or effectiveness of conflict resolution programs, including peer mediation, in schools. However, one kind of evidence has existed for years: on-the-ground educational practitioners' interest in and commitment to peer mediation has fueled the rapid spread of these innovations. Educators have voted with their feet. Thousands and thousands of new programs have been adopted and diversified in schools across Ohio (Ohio Commission on Dispute Resolution and Conflict Management, 1997) as well as across the United States, Canada, and much of the world (CREnet/ACR, 2000; Hall, 1999; Lawton, 1994; Strickland and others, 1995).

NOTE: *For more information about the Cleveland Municipal School District Center for Conflict Resolution, contact Carole Close at Cleveland Public Schools Center for Conflict Resolution, Martin Luther King High School, 1651 East Seventy-First St., Cleveland, OH 44103.*

The autonomous and student-centered nature of many peer mediation programs makes programs less systematically comparable across different sites for research purposes (Horowitz and Boardman, 1994; Moriarty and MacDonald, 1994). Until recently, there has been little funding for rigorous or cross-program research, partly because of the programs' already expanding popularity. Many of the earlier studies of school-based peer mediation and negotiation focused on small samples or single programs, without giving much attention to the programs' theoretical underpinnings, relationships with other initiatives, or fit within school contexts (Carter, 1995; Jenkins and Smith, 1995; Kalmakoff and Shaw, 1987). Although this research generally presented a positive evaluation of school-based peer mediation programs, it was unclear how applicable the results might be within other contexts.

The most pronounced impact of peer mediation programs has typically been on the student mediators themselves. These students have the most sustained opportunities to experience and practice the roles, relationships, and skills associated with this form of nonviolent problem solving (Gentry and Benenson, 1992; Lam, 1988; Shulman, 1996; Van Slyck and Stern, 1991). Diverse teams of peer mediators—including students with different levels of academic ability who represent diverse social, cultural, and gender groups—tend to improve the strength, sustainability, and effectiveness of mediation programs, as compared with more homogeneous teams (Day-Vines and others, 1996; DeJong, 1994; Schrumpf, Crawford, and Bodine, 1997).

Existing research generally agrees that where there are sufficient mediators on duty, peer mediation programs are associated with a reduction in physical aggression (Cunningham and others, 1998). Many researchers have associated peer mediation with reduction in disciplinary actions (Bodine and Crawford, 1998; Lane and McWhirter, 1992; Stomfay-Stitz, 1994). Equally important, peer mediation supports student learning of problem solving, decision making, communication skills, critical thinking, and conflict resolution and self-discipline skills (Crary, 1992; Cutrona and Guerin, 1994; Hall, 1999; Johnson and Johnson, 1996; Jones, Kmitta, and Vegso, 1998; Lane and McWhirter, 1992). Where mediator teams are diverse and bias is addressed, students may also develop intercultural sensitivity (Day-Vines and others, 1996).

The vast majority (85 to 95 percent) of student conflicts that go to peer mediation are resolved, and nearly all of those agreements are kept (Massachusetts Association of Mediation Programs, 1995). The more completely voluntary the referrals to mediation are (that is, where students have a real option to refuse such assistance without being punished), the more satisfied the disputants are with the process and the agreements reached (Jones, Kmitta, and Vegso, 1998).

Jones, Kmitta, and Vegso (1998), in the Comprehensive Peer Mediation Evaluation Project, examined programs in nine elementary schools, nine middle schools, and nine secondary schools in three U.S. cities, provided by three training organizations from which the evaluators were independent. They compared peer mediation–only programs—in which a cadre of students was trained to become mediators (comparable to CCR's program) for whole-school programs that trained a wider range of students and infused conflict resolution lessons in classroom curriculum—with comparison schools that had no special conflict resolution programs. They found that both cadre and whole-school peer mediation programs significantly benefited students and schools by improving social conflict behavior. The greatest impact of the programs was on the students who were trained directly and given opportunities to practice mediation, but the entire student population also benefited.

The Comprehensive Peer Mediation Evaluation Project has also suggested that peer mediation can improve school climate as measured by teacher and staff perceptions, although the impact on students' perceptions of the school climate was minimal. (As Cunningham and others, 1998, have shown, adults in school are often unaware of a large proportion of the violence and bullying experienced by their students.) Jones, Kmitta, and Vegso (1998) indicated that at the elementary school level, well-designed and implemented cadre programs could have as significant an effect on school climate as whole-school programs. This research improves our certainty that peer mediation programs can contribute to building safe and peaceful school environments. The present study of the CCR Elementary School Initiative (ESI) was designed to reinforce these results and to extend our qualitative understanding of the specific program interpretation and implementation practices and their consequences in urban elementary schools.

Research Context: The Cleveland Schools Center for Conflict Resolution

The Winning Against Violent Environments (WAVE) mediation program has been operating at the Martin Luther King Magnet School in the inner city of Cleveland since about 1983. In addition to mediating conflicts at their own school, youths from the WAVE program have been leading conflict resolution and peer mediation training sessions in local and distant schools and communities since about 1988. Peer mediation has been included in the Cleveland Municipal School District (CMSD) Student Handbook as an accepted alternative to traditional discipline measures for handling certain kinds of conflict. Peer mediation is also available for student conflicts that do not involve disciplinary offenses—disagreements in the schoolyard, hallway, or classroom that have not escalated into serious disruptions or violence.

In fall 1995, WAVE's conflict resolution training program was recognized and institutionalized in its own school district, and it expanded into the CMSD Center for Conflict Resolution (CCR). The program's guiding light for the past eighteen years is a specially assigned social studies teacher, Carole Close. Close and her staff, generally young people who recently graduated from Cleveland schools, subsequently developed conflict resolution and training programs for a range of contexts and grade levels (Close and Lechman, 1997).

The CMSD CCR program uses the same basic model as most school-based peer mediation programs in North America. What is most unique about the CCR program is that, first, it emphasizes empowerment, leadership, and training by the urban youths themselves, and, second, its mediation services are becoming available district-wide at several grade levels. In 1996, the Cleveland Teachers Union signed a contract with the CMSD. That contract created a position called Conflict Management Program Adviser, an extra part-time position compensated by stipend, to be held by a certified staff member in each of the district's 120 schools, contingent upon the passage of a tax levy to support the schools. In January 1997, after the levy passed, the district funded the middle school and high school components of the CCR program and assigned the CCR the responsibility of training teams of peer mediators and advisers and of helping them to establish extracurricular conflict mediation programs in these schools.

The Cleveland Summit on Education, a local foundation associated with the Greater Cleveland Roundtable, filled a gap in the school district's program implementation by funding the CCR's initial effort to extend the mediation program into elementary schools. In 1997–98, the CCR began to train the first of these new elementary school conflict management advisers and their students and to establish new peer mediation programs in about a quarter of the district's elementary schools. As part of their support for the Elementary School Conflict Resolution Initiative, the Cleveland Summit on Education sponsored this evaluation research project.

Research Project: The Elementary School Conflict Resolution Initiative

The CMSD CCR had trained many teams of elementary school conflict mediators in Cleveland before. The new element in 1997 was the institutionalization (and remuneration) of designated Conflict Management Program Advisers on each school's staff. They would be responsible for implementing CCR-designed programs at each school. Another new element, resulting from a dovetailing State of Ohio program, was that CCR was able to offer staff development to these school-based advisers—two to three released days per year. Thus the ESI supported CCR to offer its standard training program, with the addition of slightly better institutional support for professional development and school-based program development than had been available in the past.

Program design. A team of twenty-five to thirty elementary students (called conflict managers in this program) from each of twenty-eight project schools received program development assistance and an intensive three-day peer mediation training, led by CCR staff members. The training staff members were diverse youths who had recently graduated from high school in Cleveland, and they were assisted by a few current high school student mediators. One or two adult advisers (sometimes teachers working in regular classrooms and sometimes special resource teachers without their own classrooms), and often one or two parent or community volunteers, were trained at the same time, along with their student mediator teams. Groups of advisers also received a day or two of additional professional development, led by Close and the CCR training staff, regarding implementation of mediation and conflict education across their schools. The CCR directed these advisers—in consultation with colleagues at their schools—to choose as mediator trainees children whose social leadership potential had been exhibited in negative or positive ways and who were representative of the school's entire racial, cultural, and gender populations and all grade three, four, and five classrooms. Thus the CCR program emphasized youth leadership in combination with an institutionalized adult support system.

These student conflict mediators, grades three through five, and their adult advisers were trained by the CCR's youth staff to develop conflict resolution and mediation skills. At the end of the three-day training and in follow-up visits, the CCR staff encouraged the conflict managers (mediators) and advisers to take the initiative in developing unique and appropriate conflict resolution programs in their own schools.

Research Method

The research project's purpose was to study what happened in the first twelve months after each peer mediation training program was initiated, and it was then enabled to develop autonomously in several different elementary schools in the same urban school district. Specifically, I gathered quantitative and qualitative information regarding the program's implementation process and its effectiveness in training twenty to thirty students and one or more adults in each of twenty-eight schools to provide ongoing support for conflict resolution program development at each school, thereby improving the school climate and the understandings of students regarding the management of conflict. The unit of analysis in the study was the school; individual children and teachers remain anonymous. The initial research funding was awarded by the Cleveland Summit on Education, a project of the Greater Cleveland Roundtable, in August 1997; the first set of trainings began that fall. Data collection was completed in May 1999.

Sample

A diverse set of twenty Cleveland public elementary schools was initially identified for this initiative. The CCR included schools of different sizes and different program emphases, schools in all regions of the city (reflecting Cleveland's ethnic, racial, and economic diversity). Because the program was implemented "from the top" (required by the school district administration) at a time of turbulent change in the Cleveland school system, most schools were delayed in appointing staff members to be conflict management program advisers (a prerequisite to CCR training). Thus the project selected mediators and advisers from the small number of schools that were actually available to begin the program in 1997–98. Nine of the schools in this original sample had received CCR training in the past two or three years. None had fully active programs at the time of the 1997–98 Initiative Project training, although six schools had a few student mediators and/or an adviser with some CCR experience left from previous trainings. Eleven of the initial twenty schools had received no CCR training before 1997. Thus the Elementary School Conflict Resolution Initiative study sample was balanced, including some schools whose staff members were uninterested in peer mediation and had sought no CCR services in the past, as well as other schools that had joined the initiative because of their interest derived from prior exposure to CCR's program.

Because of tight school schedules and a limited number of trainers, trainings and program start-up at each school took place at different times. Thus the main project schools were coded as Phase I (year one fall semester training, posttest at the end of the fall semester in January 1999) and Phase II (year one spring semester training, posttest at the end of spring semester in May 1999). These twenty schools each had approximately one full year to implement their programs; they were the main focus of this study. For comparison purposes, a group of fourteen additional schools were given pretests in the fall of year two and posttests in May of the same year. Eight Phase III new (second-round) project schools received CCR training in the fall. Six Phase IV no-project schools, originally intended to serve as a comparison group, did not receive CCR training until after the May 1999 posttest. However, several of these schools misunderstood instructions and did begin conflict resolution education programming before the posttest; thus, this comparison group was dropped from the study.

Qualitative Evidence

Qualitative data assessed the processes, roles, character, and effectiveness of program implementation by comparing schools' climates, activities, student roles, and skills early and late in their first year of implementing the peer mediation program and by analyzing between-school differences. Observations and interviews involved adults and selected children, both directly engaged and relatively unengaged with the peer mediation program, at all twenty-eight schools (Phases I, II, and III). For more specific information on methodology, see Bickmore (2000).

Quantitative Evidence

Quantitative data focused primarily on the research question regarding program effectiveness. The major quantitative measure was an anonymous survey of grade three, four, and five students' understandings and attitudes toward conflict, which was administered preprogram and after a year of program implementation. The results of this survey were aggregated and analyzed by program phase (groups of schools), by school, by grade level, and (for some schools) by gender. The other quantitative information was routinely collected by the school board. It compared the district's average elementary school attendance rates, disciplinary suspension rates, and pass rates on grade four achievement tests with those of the phase I, II, and III project schools.

The paper-and-pencil survey, Student Attitudes About Conflict (SAAC), is an adapted version of a survey created by the New Mexico Center for Dispute Resolution (Jenkins and Smith, 1995; see also Bickmore, 2000, for full details on measurement). It was administered twice (as pretest and posttest) by teachers in their own classrooms, to approximately four thousand students each time, grades three through five, at each of thirty-four schools (twenty main project schools, eight second-round new project schools, and six no-project comparison schools). Overall program effectiveness was assessed by comparing the amounts average; SAAC scores changed after each school had implemented the CCR program for a year.

The adapted SAAC survey has four subscales—groupings of questions that together describe particular aspects of students' understandings and attitudes toward conflict and their potential for success in school. Each of these themes has been identified in previous research as a potential outcome of peer mediation programming. The four thematic subscales are

- CR—Understanding of conflict resolution and problem solving indicates understanding of the conflict and the inclination to handle it nonviolently.

- PR—Peer relationships and the concept of one's own social skills indicates a student's self-assessment of his or her capacity to handle conflict and get along with other people.

- SA—School attachment, comfort, and commitment in school indicates a student's attitude toward attending and participating in school.

- SC—Perception of school climate and safety at school indicates a student's assessment of the level of safety in his or her school environment.

Additional quantitative evidence was derived from routinely collected public records of the CMSD. Because prior research indicates that peer mediation can improve students' attitudes toward school, this research assessed average attendance rates at project schools. Because prior research indicates that peer mediation can help students improve academically relevant skills, this research assessed Ohio Proficiency Test pass rates for grade four in the two subjects most closely related to peer mediation—reading and citizenship. Because prior research associates peer mediation with reducing violence, this research assessed suspension rates (in elementary school contexts, suspensions are punishment for violent behavior). For each of these indicators, CCR project schools (in phases according to the training date) were compared with the CMSD's elementary school averages in 1996–97 (immediately preceding implementation of the ESI) and in 1998–99 (the end of year two of the initiative).

Results: Analysis of Qualitative Evidence

The qualitative data were rich in information about best practices and areas of needed improvement.

Training, Program Interpretation and Scope, Roles of Participants, and Sustainability

Interviews with direct participants in the CCR program and with other members of each school community, as well as on-site observations, yielded information regarding strengths, weaknesses, and innovative approaches to CCR program implementation at the school level. This section reports on triangulated cross-case analysis to highlight general results and implementation themes across the twenty-eight schools in the CCR ESI.

Clearly there remain significant challenges in reliably developing and institutionalizing peer mediation programs in elementary schools such as those in Cleveland. Half to two-thirds of the twenty original project schools demonstrated significant program development between years one and two. Others did well only in year two, after accomplishing essentially no program development in the project's first year. Some developed well in year one but did not sustain strong programs in year two. CCR, at its current level of staffing, was extremely dependent on the commitment and capacity of each school-based conflict management program adviser and administrator to implement and develop the peer mediation programs and to influence other adults and students in their schools to support student-centered conflict resolution activity.

Training and Follow-Up by Youth and Adult Leaders: CCR Staff Services

More than seven hundred elementary students and more than forty adults (program advisers and volunteers) were trained in this initiative at the twenty-eight Phase I, II, and III schools. In addition to leading the three-day

trainings of peer mediation teams at each school, the young CCR ESI training staff (recent high school graduates)

- Carried out at least one follow-up visit to each school and adviser
- Made presentations at school staff meetings
- Led workshops for parent groups at some project schools
- Assisted CCR's program coordinator, Carole Close, in conducting
  professional development for all conflict management program
  advisers as a group
- Assisted Close in identifying and disseminating materials for schools
  to use to facilitate integrating conflict resolution throughout
  classroom work and school environments

Written evaluations of individual student mediators' skills by CCR staff
members at the end of each three-day training, as well as oral descriptions
by school-based program advisers and classroom teachers, indicate that
nearly all the students CCR trained developed fair or good proficiency in
the steps and underlying conflict management skills of peer mediation.

Many of the student mediators who were CCR trained were strong
enough to, in turn, influence the understandings and openness of many of
their peers to nonviolent conflict management. In contrast, in the five or
six schools where on-site research visits revealed that adult advisers had
trained some additional mediators themselves (contrary to CCR guidelines), those new mediators' skills and enthusiasm were distinctly uneven
and, on average, considerably weaker than those of the students trained by
the CCR staff. Beyond their evident skill in mediation, CCR trainers were
unusually effective role models because they (like their young trainees)
were diverse young people who grew up and studied in the CMSD.

Clearly the young mediators and their advisers had been exposed over
many years, in school and out, to society's prevailing models of conflict
management, including arbitration (judging), advising, and punishing.
Although CCR promoted an alternate form of dispute resolution—one
in which the third-party helper wields far less substantive authority or
punitive power than a judge, principal, or counselor would, at times their
training was not strong enough to clarify the differences between peer
mediation and these more directive approaches to conflict. An important
instance of this misunderstanding was that in four or five of the original
twenty project schools, the conflict management program adviser added a

ground rule (contrary to CCR guidelines) that participants should "tell the truth," and sometimes he or she even involved additional people in mediation sessions as "witnesses." This transformed mediation from a participant-centered effort emphasizing present and future problem solving to a backward-looking effort emphasizing placement of blame.

The most frequently mentioned additional request by school staffs was that CCR update and extend the information they disseminated regarding linkages between conflict resolution and academic learning. Although this research shows that peer mediation is positively associated with academic achievement (see the section on quantitative analysis), the strategies for enhancing that connection—effectively using conflict resolution and peer mediation to strengthen on-task behavior and academic skill building and effectively using academic learning activities to strengthen conflict resolution—need to be further explained and practiced in professional development initiatives. This seems to be one conflict resolution education task that can best be handled by professional certified teachers rather than by youth trainers.

School-Site Program Development and Institutionalization: Administrator and Staff Roles

Through the efforts of the CCR staff, student mediators, and staff members in each school, the CCR ESI met its goal of influencing a significant proportion of the grade three through five student population in most project schools. In about six of the twenty main project schools, a robust majority of grade three through five students, when observed and orally assessed in their classrooms, showed significant familiarity with the purpose and process of peer mediation. In an additional eight or nine schools, a sizeable minority of the grade three through five student population were well informed about mediation. In five schools, significant proportions of grade one and two students, in addition to grades three through five, were well informed about mediation. Clearly these programs had developed considerably beyond the original small cadres of mediators that were directly trained by CCR.

In fifteen of twenty schools, between 5 and 50 percent of the grade three through five students reported having received direct assistance from peer mediators in resolving interpersonal conflicts during the past year. In those fifteen schools, by spring 1999, between one and six or more peer mediation sessions per week were being conducted. About half of the twenty programs showed quite extensive program growth and development between spring 1998 (project year one) and spring 1999 (project year two), and about four others showed slower, but evident, program development. Schools that were implementing CCR programs for the first time showed more positive initial growth during the assessed year than schools that had already received some CCR training services before this project's pretests. This indicates that more than one year is generally needed for full program implementation.

The CCR program was admired by students: over 70 percent of the grade three through five students who were not already conflict managers (from 50 percent to over 90 percent at various project schools) indicated on SAAC surveys that they would like to be conflict managers. In the classrooms visited during on-site observations, the percentages of students who indicated they wanted to be conflict managers were similarly high. Although a less representative sample, these on-site results substantiate the reliability of these data, because I asked the question immediately after reviewing with the class what conflict managers did.

CCR programs at all schools negotiated the multiple pressures and competing priorities that face urban schools today. Principals in Cleveland during the project period carried a great deal of this pressure, partly due to the ways they were accountable for their students' Ohio Proficiency Test scores. One rough indicator of this pressure's effect on students from relating qualitative to quantitative data is the SAAC "school attachment" result for the students in grades four and five, for whom the proficiency test was a major element of either the first or second project year. Where principals and school staffs supported peer mediation activity, even during the achievement test preparation period, their schools generally showed more improvement in grade four and five students' school attachment and program development than those who allowed test preparation to interfere with student-centered extracurricular learning activity, such as peer mediation.

Time-tabling regular meetings was the single most tangible and effective way for schools to show their commitment and facilitate the success of peer mediation. Programs that met during school, every week, during a designated period were considerably more successful than programs that met after school or that met less often than every other week. In particular, student mediators who were not already successful in other aspects of school (including discipline matters), and those whose English-language communication skills were weak, truly needed the consistent encouragement, support, and practice of regular conflict management team meetings. When programs did not meet frequently, these students in particular tended to drop out, to be kicked out for misbehavior, or to become inactive as peer mediators. When mediation teams thereby became less heterogeneous and less representative of the student body, programs tended to stagnate or to not influence the skills and behavior of their school populations. When principals and union representatives (who set timetables) allocated even one regular period per week, it made a world of difference.

Relating mediation to discipline policy was also crucial. School-based initiatives were more successful when they developed and communicated to all staff members a clear, noncoercive policy regarding the prerequisites, consequences, and procedures for using peer mediation, as distinct from more top-down discipline procedures. Program effects were strengthened when teachers and administrators modeled respect for the program by referring students to it (that is, suggesting that they use peer mediation to address their problems). At the same time, the power of the mediation alternative rests on its voluntary, confidential, and nonpunitive nature. Situations involving serious physical violence would typically not be mediated by students in any case, especially at the elementary level. In schools that treated students' minor interpersonal conflicts as punishable offenses and presented them with the loaded "choice" to use mediation or be punished, the voluntary nature of peer mediation was undercut and its effectiveness suffered. For example, a few schools that discouraged or punished students for using mediation "too much" were implicitly teaching those students not to seek help in taking responsibility to nonviolently resolve their problems and was preventing them from practicing skills that they evidently needed. Where conflict management program advisers served on school discipline or safety committees, or in some way were able to regularly communicate with colleagues about appropriate conflicts to refer to mediation (distinguishing this from punishment), their schools showed more successful results from the CCR program.

Program Development and Institutionalization: Program Advisers' Roles

Conflict Management Program Advisers in each school had three main responsibilities:

1. Meeting regularly with conflict managers for skill practice, debriefing, and analysis of their mediation challenges and doing group planning regarding conflict management program development

2. Facilitating the duty schedules and referral process for getting mediators connected to conflict situations, including assigning appropriate partners, giving all mediators equitable opportunities to offer their services, and following up where needed with mediators and/or clients

3. Leading conflict management program development, including disseminating information, resources, and motivation to all members of the school, by initiating formal and informal learning activities and by facilitating peer mediator decision making and coleadership of the program

To make peer mediation a viable alternative in the school, advisers had to conduct program-related activities during their already-busy school day—when students, staff members, and others were present. Advisers were also essential links to the professional teaching staff, clarifying and enhancing links between conflict mediation and academic work. Because the role of Conflict Management Program Adviser was new in the Cleveland District in year one of the Elementary School Conflict Resolution Initiative (1997–98), many administrators had little prior knowledge that would have helped them to choose good advisers for the CCR program. Thus it is remarkable that the majority of advisers did fairly well in implementing peer mediation programs in their schools. Because they were professional educators working in their own schools, these advisers were well suited to interpret and adapt peer mediation to fit the particular populations, program priorities, schedules, and staffing strengths of their schools.

Program Interpretation: Student Mediators' Roles, Participation, and Diversity

Some schools were far more successful than others in sustaining the involvement of diverse student mediators, especially those originally seen as "negative leaders" and those whose first language was not English. They were active and confident members of the program. Where diverse mediator teams were sustained, the most important factor was the commitment and capacity of the program advisers to coach, support, and encourage the whole range of students. Advisers' and other staff members' ongoing support for all mediators' learning and second chances was somewhat inadequate in many schools. In programs with regular and frequent conflict manager meetings, better diversity was maintained and thus programs were better able to influence their schools. Where student mediators had input into policy regarding the consequences of their own behavior, programs were better able to avoid the restriction of mediation to a narrow "good student" population.

In many of the same schools that emphasized the monitor or model roles for student mediators, it was common for quite a large number of mediators to lose interest in or be kicked out of the program. Such programs no longer had sufficient numbers of student mediators representing all of the school's population subgroups. Because boys are generally somewhat more likely to get into physical fights (and to get punished for their conflict behavior), several of the schools' conflict manager groups have become predominately female—sometimes disproportionately white. This narrowing in mediator team diversity communicated to student populations that mediation was not necessarily for everybody, and it caused some people to avoid or not try mediation. In schools where staff members had developed clear policies for handling problems and supporting diverse mediators, more—and more varied—student mediators remained active and effective.

In virtually every case where they were given support, respect, and opportunities to show what they could do, the grade three through five student mediators in this project met and exceeded the expectations of those around them. The enthusiastic testimonials from formerly skeptical teachers, administrators, peers, and parents indicate that young children can indeed help build peaceful environments. The longer and more widely a program developed in a school, the more enthusiasm these young peacemakers generated. The positive school effects shown in this study result from the fact that these young people were able to influence a great number of their peers toward nonviolent inclinations and relationships. In some schools, conflict manager activity involved primarily mediation per se. In others, conflict managers applied their skills in a wider range of ways—for example, making presentations to peers and parents regarding mediation and conflict. The only serious lament I heard about the program from student mediators in any of the twenty-eight CCR project schools occurred where they were not given the opportunity to be sufficiently active, to show what they could do to make their schools more safe and peaceful.

Quantitative Analysis

Quantitative data focused primarily on the results of the CCR's program effectiveness.

Student Attitudes About Conflict Survey Results

Overall. Prepost comparisons of SAAC survey results show that the CCR's elementary conflict management program had, on average, small but significant positive results, even after only one year of implementation. Results are reported here for the fourteen main project schools that implemented the program and provided valid data (Bickmore, 2000, includes full information on all project schools). Average posttest scores in schools that implemented the program were higher than pretest scores on the survey taken as a whole and on three of the four thematic subscales (see Table 1). The overall incremental improvement between the pretest and the posttest averaged across all implemented Phase I and II schools was significant statistically ('T-test' $p < 0.01$).

The CCR program is associated with improvements in students' understanding and inclination toward nonviolent conflict resolution (the CR scale), and with improvements in students' assessment of their own capacity to handle conflicts in interactions with peers (the PR scale). This indicates that, on average, the understandings and feelings of efficacy to handle conflict increased in the grades three through five student populations of CCR project schools. Students' attitudes toward attending and participating in school (the SA scale) also improved significantly. This indicates that the existence of CCR peer mediation programs helps to improve the average student's comfort with engaging in school activities. These results reflect school-level improvements in students' capacities and willingness to handle effectively both interpersonal relationships and school activities.

One year of program implementation was not sufficient to show a highly significant improvement in school climate as perceived by the

Table 1. Implementation for Phase 1 and 2 Main Project Schools: The Mean Prepost Difference by Grade and Subscale

(N = 14)	All Grades	Grade 3	Grade 4	Grade 5	Conflict Managers
School climate	0.06*	0.04	0.05	0.14*	0.08
Peer relations	0.08***	0.07	0.07*	0.12**	0.06
Conflict resolution	0.10***	0.17***	0.03	0.13**	0.14**
School attachment	0.11***	0.19***	0.10**	0.09*	0.11**
All scales	0.09***	0.13***	0.06*	0.12**	0.10**

*$p \leq 0.10$.
**$p \leq 0.05$.
***$p \leq 0.01$.

average student (the SC scale). Students' average perception of their school climate was relatively negative before implementation of the CCR project; it was more varied (higher standard deviation), but, on average, it was little better after a year of this project. The incidence of name calling reported by many students was particularly high in most schools. The schools with better overall program implementation (as assessed by qualitative measures) did achieve generally better school climate results. This suggests that when CCR peer mediation programs achieve full implementation (normally after about three years), school climates may indeed be improved.

The CCR mediation program improves the average student's school experience in grades three through five as well as their consequent learning to handle conflict and human relationships, to a limited but significant degree. As would be expected when averaging survey scores from thousands of diverse children early in the program implementation process, the overall program increases from pretest to posttest are not large (approximately one-tenth of one step on the five-point survey scale). Also, the degree of variation among students' results is sometimes fairly high (standard deviations of 0.34–0.95 across schools, overall and by grade level). This indicates that the CCR program was not equally effective for all children (nor for all grades or all schools). "Cadre" mediation programs, especially in early stages of program development when they are only partially implemented, are unlikely to serve all students equally. Variation among students, as well as among schools (standard deviation), was highest in the school climate subscale. This means that significant numbers of students continued to experience their schools as being somewhat unsafe. To sufficiently change the behavior of enough students—to make even the least popular students feel completely safe in school—would require a longer and more comprehensive program than the one-year peer mediation program studied here. Nonetheless, the average SAAC score increases—across the large number of diverse students and schools assessed—show that the CCR ESI positively affected most students in most schools.

Conflict managers (peer mediators). Seen less consistently than had been shown in previous research, conflict managers sometimes had stronger results than their schools as a whole. However, the substantial between-school differences in peer mediator results exceeded the between-group differences across the various program schools. In schools whose conflict managers were relatively inactive (according to qualitative data), conflict managers had lower SAAC score improvements than their peers. Because of their special responsibilities as mediators, conflict managers became exceptionally aware of peer conflict in their schools and thus tended to show a particularly strong "implementation dip" in conflict awareness. In more active and inclusive programs, peer mediators received more opportunity to learn and internalize conflict resolution skills through training, and then, by advocating them among peers, they achieved stronger results.

Grade levels. The average results for students in grades three through five are much stronger than they are for students in grade four. This is because many students in grade four were denied opportunities to participate fully in this program by teachers or principals, on the assumption that such activity would be detrimental to Ohio Proficiency Test results (an incorrect assumption). In the schools where grade four students were allowed to participate as actively as other students, their results were comparable to those of students in other grades. The between-grade differences varied widely from school to school, depending on which students were given the most opportunities to participate in conflict resolution activity. This confirms that children as young as those in grade three can benefit from peer mediation if given well-supported opportunities to participate. Grade three students (at the time of the posttest in program year two) would not have received direct training from the CCR staff. Their strong results, even more than those of students in other grades, are the result of program implementation beyond the original peer mediator cadres in their schools.

Between-school (program implementation) differences. The data for the eighteen project schools analyzed quantitatively show tremendous between-school differences in program results (Bickmore, 2000). These quantitative results are reinforced and explained by qualitative data from all twenty-eight schools, which indicates that the individual school's interpretation and implementation of the peer mediation program is at least as important as the program model itself in determining program effectiveness.

Quantitative Measures Using Cleveland Municipal School District Data: Attendance, Suspension, and Academic Achievement

Information collected by the CMSD also provides support for the effectiveness of the CCR elementary conflict management program. Table 2 presents comparisons between the academic year 1996–97 (spring preceding project implementation) and the academic year 1998–99 (the final spring of the evaluation project).

Students' increased feelings of attachment to school (demonstrated by SAAC survey results) were not sufficient to increase the average attendance

Table 2. Change of Percentage in Information Collected by the District from 1996–97 Through 1998–99

Program Averages	Attendance Rate	Reading Pass Rate	Citizenship Pass Rate	#Suspensions
Fall training (early phase I)	−0.1	+26.1*	+34.3*	−36.1*
Spring training (late phase I and phase II)	−0.1	+54.4**	+63.0***	−13.2
Phase III	−0.9	+41.7**	+79.9***	+34.7
Implemented Phase I and II (N = 14)	−0.1	+37.2**	+45.4***	−24.9
Whole district (elem.)	+2.1	+22.8	+38.1	+2.1

*p ≤ 0.10.
**p ≤ 0.05.
***p ≤ 0.01.

rates at most CCR project schools. Too many other variables influence students' school attendance, especially at the elementary level.

Suspension rates were considerably reduced in CCR project schools, compared with the average district elementary school, during the project period. Whereas Cleveland's overall average elementary school suspension rate (a consequence of violent behavior) went *up* by about 2 percent, suspension rates in the main CCR project schools (implemented Phase I and II) went *down* by an average of 25 percent (improving most in fall-trained schools). The between-school variation was high enough to prevent statistical significance on this variable, except for slightly in the case of CCR schools trained in the fall, partly because CCR schools are also included in the district averages. Peer mediation provides a meaningful alternative to suspension by resolving problems—rather than by simply punishing—and by helping children learn alternative ways to handle their conflicts.

Pass rates on the grade four Ohio Proficiency Tests of citizenship and reading increased in CCR project schools considerably more than the district average. Conflict resolution education and practice is a good way to improve communication and language skills (reflected in the reading test) as well as understandings of problem solving and community processes (reflected in the citizenship test). This supports the claim that time spent outside regular class for extracurricular activities, such as CCR's peer mediation program, can increase students' academically relevant skills and their comfort in school and help them resolve personal problems so that they can focus on learning (see also Williams, 1992).

Study Limitations and Future Research Needed

A strength of this study is the triangulated data gathered from youth trainers from the same community as project schools and from large numbers of diverse students, diverse adult stakeholders, and diverse schools (all trained with the same basic program model), throughout a year per school. However, quantitative data would have been much more reliable if there were valid data from a no-program comparison group and if adequate funding allowed direct, controlled administration of surveys (rather than delegating survey responsibilities to program advisers in each school, which caused a lot of incorrectly gathered data to be wasted). Thus, while the robust sample size and multiphase design strengthen the SAAC evidence, these results must be treated with caution, as they are partly artifacts of context and timing. Also, one year is clearly not sufficient for full implementation (including diffusion of effects throughout a school) of peer mediation programs. Future research should examine program implementation in depth over the several years required for full program development.

Conclusions and Recommendations

What (and how much) effect does the CCR ESI peer mediation program have on the school environment as a whole, especially on the grade three through five student population, in a range of different school settings? This research points clearly toward the effectiveness of peer mediation programming in elementary schools and specifically toward the effective work of the CMSD CCR in initiating, training, and developing such programs in diverse Cleveland elementary schools. In spite of the relatively short duration of the study period, limited funding, and the getting started glitches of the new adviser roles in the schools, the ESI was successful. Many of the areas for improvement that were highlighted by the research can be solved with strengthened funding and a sustained period of reflective practice.

What factors and stakeholders facilitate or impede effective implementation of an elementary school peer mediation program in this northern U.S. inner-city context? What most needs improvement is the development and maintenance of sustainable programs at the school level. This will require some improvement in CCR professional development and resource materials for program development, including dissemination of information to administrators, teacher's union representatives, and staffs (including Conflict Management Program Advisers) at each school. Resources that enhance dovetailing between conflict resolution and academic learning goals are particularly essential. The clear consensus among staff members and students at virtually all project schools was that funding was needed to allow for more extensive, equitably distributed, thorough, and frequent follow-up support by the CCR staff at each school site. In addition, district- and school-level administrators and union leaders can do a great deal to institutionalize peer mediation as a regular component of the academic curriculum and the whole school environment by making space for the work of conflict managers in the timetable, in meetings with students, in staff meetings, in professional development time, and in the regular activity of classrooms.

At a minimum, one period per week during school should be scheduled for peer mediator meetings with their adviser at a regular time when all can attend. Conflict resolution programming is as important as any other special class or learning activity, and allocating time is the most concrete and useful demonstration of a school administration and staff's commitment to the success of diverse students in the peer mediation program. Wherever possible, an additional period or more per week should be allocated for Conflict Management Program Advisers to work on program development and planning with the staff and with parent/neighborhood communities. It is appropriate for a large part of an extra-stipend job to be carried out in a staff member's "own" time, but sufficient funding is necessary to make it possible for the adviser to do some work during school, when colleagues and students are present.

Leadership and information dissemination are necessary—in particular, to clarify the differences and intersections between the peer mediation alternative and the regular discipline patterns and program priorities of the school. Peer mediation cannot work well if it is entwined in a highly restrictive or coercive environment: students' relative autonomy, voluntary participation, and confidentiality must be ensured for such programs to thrive. Leadership is also necessary to ensure equitable participation in the peer mediation program. Diverse teams of conflict managers, who can improve the school experiences of whole school populations, are not sustainable without clear, conscious, and consistent support by the CCR staff in follow-up work, by Conflict Management Program Advisers, and by school administrators and staffs. No adviser can do this alone; he or she may need coadvisers, a Conflict Management Committee, or some other clear tie into the staff committee and work structure of the school.

In summary, the results of this research affirm that cadre-type peer mediation programs can improve elementary students' capacity and inclination to handle conflict nonviolently, improve their relationships with their peers, and increase their attachment to the school. Furthermore, such a program can reduce suspensions from school for violent activity and can increase achievement in reading and citizenship. The CCR's training and program model is sound and workable and its training and program advisory staff members have done good work with limited funding. At the same time, good training is not enough. School-based program development and support to build programs that can grow and last over time will require strengthened commitment and clarity of purpose at the CCR, at each school, and across the CMSD.

References

Bickmore, K. *Evaluation Research Report: Cleveland Municipal School District Center for Conflict Resolution Elementary School Conflict Resolution Initiative Peer Mediation Training and Program Implementation.* Available from Ohio Commission on Dispute Resolution and Conflict Management. [http://www.state.oh.us/cdr.] 2000.

Bodine, R. J., and Crawford, D. J. *The Handbook of Conflict Resolution Education: A Guide to Building Quality Schools.* San Francisco: National Institute for Dispute Resolution and Jossey-Bass, 1998.

Carter, S. L. *School Mediation Evaluation Report.* Albuquerque: New Mexico Center for Dispute Resolution, 1995.

Close, C., and Lechman, K. "Fostering Youth Leadership: Students Train Students and Adults in Conflict Resolution." *Theory Into Practice,* 1997, *36* (1), 11–16.

Crary, D. R. "Community Benefits from Mediation: A Test of the 'Peace Virus' Hypothesis." *Mediation Quarterly,* 1992, *9* (3), 241–252.

CREnet/ACR. "What Is Conflict Resolution in Education?" Washington, D.C.: Conflict Resolution Educators Network. CREnet has since become part of the Association for Conflict Resolution. [http://www.acresolution.org]. June 2000.

Cunningham, C., and others. "The Effects of Primary Division, Student-Mediated Conflict Resolution Programs on Playground Aggression." *Journal of Child Psychology and Psychiatry,* 1998, *39* (5), 653–662.

Cutrona, C., and Guerin, D. "Confronting Conflict Peacefully." *Educational Horizons,* 1994 (Winter), 95–104.

Day-Vines, N., and others. "Conflict Resolution: The Value of Diversity in the Recruitment, Selection, and Training of Peer Mediators." *School Counselor,* 1996, *43* (May), 392–410.

DeJong, W. "School-Based Violence Prevention: From the Peaceable School to the Peaceable Neighborhood." *NIDR Forum,* 1994, *25,* 8–14.

Gentry, D., and Benenson, W. "School-Age Peer Mediators Transfer Knowledge and Skills to the Home Setting." *Mediation Quarterly,* 1992, *10,* 101–109.

Hall, R. "Learning Conflict Management Through Peer Mediation." In A. Raviv, L. Oppenheimer, and D. Bar-Tal (eds.), *How Children Understand War and Peace.* San Francisco: Jossey-Bass, 1999.

Horowitz, S., and Boardman, S. "Managing Conflict: Policy and Research Implications." *Journal of Social Issues,* 1994, *50* (1), 197–211.

Jenkins, J., and M. Smith. *School Mediation Evaluation Materials.* Albuquerque: New Mexico Center for Dispute Resolution, 1995.

Johnson, D., and Johnson, R. "Conflict Resolution and Peer Mediation Programs in Elementary and Secondary Schools: A Review of the Research." *Review of Educational Research,* 1996, *66* (4), 459–506.

Jones, T., Kmitta, D., and Vegso, B. "An Abbreviated Report of the Comprehensive Peer Mediation Evaluation Project." Paper presented at the annual meeting of the American Educational Research Association, San Diego, Calif., Apr. 1998.

Kalmakoff, S., and Shaw, J. *Final Report on the School Peacemakers Education Project.* Burnaby, British Columbia, Canada: School Peacemakers Education Project, 1987.

Lam, J. *The Impact of Conflict Resolution Programs on Schools.* Amherst, Mass.: National Association for Mediation in Education, 1988.

Lane, R., and McWhirter, J. "A Peer Mediation Model: Conflict Resolution for Elementary and Middle School Children." *Elementary School Guidance and Counseling,* 1992, *27* (1), 15–23.

Lawton, M. "Violence-Prevention Curricula: What Works Best?" *Education Week,* Nov. 9, 1994, 1 and 10–11.

Massachusetts Association of Mediation Programs. *A is for Alternatives to Violence: A Primer for Peer Mediation Program Training and Resources.* Boston: Massachusetts Association of Mediation Programs, n.d., circa 1995.

Moriarty, A., and McDonald, S. "How Peer Mediation Helps Students Resolve Real-Life Conflicts." In J. Wolowic (ed.), *Everybody Wins: Mediation in the Schools.* Chicago: American Bar Association, 1994. (ED 375 046)

Ohio Commission on Dispute Resolution and Conflict Management. *Conflict Management Programs in Ohio Elementary Schools: Case Studies and Evaluations.* Columbus: Ohio Commission on Dispute Resolution and Conflict Management and Ohio Department of Education, 1997.

Schrumpf, F., Crawford, D., and Bodine, R. *Peer Mediation: Conflict Resolution in Schools.* (2nd ed.) Champaign, Ill.: Research Press, 1997.

Shulman, H. "Using Developmental Principles in Violence Prevention." *Elementary School Guidance and Counseling,* 1996, *30* (Feb.), 170–175.

Stomfay-Stitz, A. "Conflict Resolution and Peer Mediation: Pathways to Safer Schools." *Childhood Education,* 1994, *70,* 279–282.

Strickland, S., and others. *Conflict Resolution in Urban American School Systems.* Washington, D.C.: National Peace Foundation, 1995.

Van Slyck, M., and Stern, M. "Conflict Resolution in Educational Settings: Assessing the Impact of Peer Mediation Programs." In K. Duffy, P. Olczak, and J. Grosch (eds.), *The Art and Science of Community Mediation.* New York: Guilford Press, 1991.

Williams, R. "The Impact of Field Education on Student Development: Research Findings." *Journal of Cooperative Education,* 1992, *27* (2), 29–45.

Kathy Bickmore is an associate professor in curriculum and sociology/equity studies at the Ontario Institute for Studies in Education, University of Toronto, Canada, and an Association for Conflict Resolution board member. She teaches graduate and teacher education and conducts research regarding education for constructive conflict, conflict resolution, equity, and inclusive democracy in public school contexts.

Structural Sources of Conflict in a University Context

ALLAN EDWARD BARSKY

Universities present an interesting setting for the analysis of conflict because of their unique organizational structures. They combine hierarchical administration with a peer philosophy that views professors as self-governing colleagues (or a community of scholars), a tenure system for job security, an ethic of academic freedom within a highly regulated and bureaucratized system, decentralized departments that often operate independently rather than as part of an organization, and myriad constituencies served by the university (Baldridge, 1971; Douglas, 1998; Hartman, 1977; Ostar, 1995).

This ethnographic study has explored experiences of conflict from the perspective of university students, professors—including both tenure- and non-tenure-stream faculty members, administrators, and support staff members. Accordingly, the purposes of this article are to (1) describe the manner in which structural factors lead to the expression of conflict within a university setting and (2) describe the implications of structural sources of conflict, including ways in which universities and other organizations can try to address these sources of conflict.

NOTE: *This article is based, in part, on a paper presented at the National Conference on Peacemaking and Conflict Resolutions, George Mason University, Fairfax, Va., June 8, 2001.*

Acknowledgments to other members of the University of Calgary Conflict Research, Resolution and Education Group (CRREG)—Jonnette Watson Hamilton, Shirley Voyna Wilson, Betty Donaldson, Anne Stalker, Terry Wigley, Jenny Geary, Laurel DiMarzo, Dani Gibson, Heather Good, Pam Klein, Jane Mitchell, Kathy Austin, Kathy Green, and Dara Neundorf-Taylor—for their insightful contributions to this project. Wigley, who was an active and dedicated community member of the research group, passed away in 2001. Also, CRREG was disbanded as a formal research group in January 2001, though some members have continued to work together on this research.

From a theoretical perspective, the dynamics of conflict in universities have been explored from the perspectives of economics, political science, industrial relations, social theory, organization, theory, psychology, and game theory (Hartman, 1977). Although some theorists have studied universities by using the same conceptual models as the ones used for other types of organizations, most agree that the university is a unique context. In contrast with most for-profit businesses, for example, universities are not typical bureaucratic structures with a single hierarchical structure. University organizational structures encompass a matrix of horizontal and vertical elements as lines of authority, decision making, and accountability cut across colleges, departments, institutes, projects, and disciplines in often overlapping and conflicting manners (Hartman, 1977).

Holton (1998) identifies three sources of conflict that, though not exclusive to universities, have a different quality or intensity of influence in this environment: incompatible goals, scarce resources, and interference from others. Given the diverse nature of different disciplines and departments, disparate purposes and goals among academic units provide an inherent source of conflict within universities. Arguably, a university is not a single organization or system but rather a complex coalition of smaller organizations. Although universities often carry an overarching mission regarding the generation of knowledge and excellence in teaching, learning, and service, each unit may have its own definition of these missions and sense of the priority these missions should receive. Warters (2000) concurs, noting that universities suffer from goal ambiguity.

In terms of perceived interference from others, Holton (1998) contends that the recent perception of scarce resources in higher education is another source of conflict. Misperception of funding fosters unnecessary competition between departments for resources. Since the 1980s, when governments began imposing more financial restraints on publicly funded universities, many universities have become more susceptible to external, political, economic, and demographic variables that compromise their internal ability to make decisions. When it comes to dealing with scarce resources, Sproule-Jones (1998) suggests that faculty members, students, and administrators can be divided into two groups: (1) equity seekers who are seeking reallocation of resources to those in need and (2) those (who are in the majority) who seek to preserve or extend their privileged positions within the university.

Warters (2000) contends that the sources of conflict within higher education settings are distinguished by the fact that there are three very distinct client groups: students, faculty members, and administrators. The present research considers an additional client group: support staff members. The characteristics of these groups and the relationships between them are inherent in the issues of conflict. The relationship between faculty members and students in higher education settings is unique in that it embraces a level of trust and dependency that does not exist in relationships in other types of organizations (Schneider, 1987, as cited in Fitzgerald, 1992). Given the principles of academic freedom and collegial administration, faculty members demand a high degree of control in decision-making processes.

Ostar (1995) suggests that conflict in universities is exacerbated not just by the fact that there are different client groups but also by the fact that each constituency claims ownership. Faculty members claim ownership by virtue of policies and pronouncements that a university is a community of scholars. Students claim ownership by virtue of the fact that they pay increasingly higher tuitions and because they believe that universities would not exist without them. Alumni claim ownership as universities seek their support financially and request their ongoing participation in university affairs. Governing boards claim ownership by virtue of their legal authority for policymaking, the hiring and firing of presidents, and budgets, even though they claim to share governance responsibility. Each subculture within the university holds its own myths about its stature within the university. Although there is some truth to each myth, the limitations of myths act as sources of conflict (Bean, 1976).

The literature on specific types of conflict resolution services at universities includes descriptions and evaluations of harassment programs (Fitzgerald, 1992; Rowe, 1990b), ombudspeople (Fuller, 1996; Harper and Rifkind, 1992; Rowe, 1990a), diversity initiatives (Volpe and Witherspoon, 1992), mediation (Warters, 2000), dispute resolution centers (Jameson, 1998), conflict resolution courses (Lewicki, 1998), and academic grievance procedures (Ludeman, 1989). A number of universities, faced with expensive lawsuits, labor strikes, grievances, and negative media attention, have been looking for more proactive and holistic approaches to conflict.

In spite of the conflict resolution programs and how-to guides that have been developed for universities, there still exists no consensus about the primary sources of conflict within this type of setting. The present study takes a step back from conflict resolution and explores structural factors that lead to conflict. By gaining a better understanding of the sources of conflict within a particular context, university decision makers can target resources and develop conflict resolution processes in a more strategic manner.

Methods

This study used a qualitative (ethnographic) research design to study the experiences of the research participants and the meanings derived from those experiences (Mertens, 1998). The sample was drawn from four groups within a large Canadian university: students (undergraduate and graduate), professors, administrators, and support staff members (including all university employees other than professors and administrators). Professors, administrators, and support staff members were randomly selected from the telephone directory of the university. Students were randomly selected from the on-line e-mail directory. All four groups were invited to participate in face-to-face interviews. The acceptance rate for interviews was highest among administrators (with six out of the eleven people invited agreeing to participate), and it was lowest among students (with 9 out of 176 invitees agreeing to participate). Administrators may have been most likely to see conflict resolution as part of their role, and the results of this research directly related to their work. Students were contacted by e-mail rather than by telephone because there was no telephone directory for all students. Although all students were assigned e-mail addresses by the university, many students did not use e-mail regularly, and the majority of students invited did not provide any response for not participating. Among professors, eleven of sixty-three invitees agreed to be interviewed. Among the support staff members, ten of twenty-eight agreed to be interviewed. The sample of interviewees reflected substantial diversity, including people of Asian, Native American, Middle Eastern, and European backgrounds, undergraduate and graduate students, professors and instructors of all the ranks—including untenured professors, and representation from over twenty-four different departments.

Four graduate social work students with extensive interviewing experience were used to conduct the interviews. Each interview lasted forty-five to ninety minutes (with an average of over sixty minutes), asking participants to describe their experiences of conflict within the university context. Interviewers explored the participants' perceptions of (1) how each conflict emerged, (2) what factors contributed to the development of the conflict, (3) how the conflict was handled, and (4) the consequences of the conflict.

Interviews were audiotaped and transcribed to allow for analysis using Atlas TI software. Atlas enabled the researchers to conduct a systematic, comprehensive, and inductive analysis of the data, identifying both uncommon and common themes pertaining to the sources of conflict in the university. The software permitted the researchers to tag and select narrative data for analysis based on first- and second-level themes, as well as allowing them to tag and select data attributable to each group.

The primary limitations of this study relate to the dependability of the information collected and the methods of sampling. Given that the interview topics pertained to conflict situations, some participants were apprehensive about discussing certain issues. They were concerned about confidentiality, were uncomfortable about discussing emotionally troubling topics, and feared retribution if others discovered what they had shared about specific conflicts. Interviewers attempted to allay these concerns by promising confidentiality, offering to conduct interviews off campus, and using data recording methods that allowed interviewees to remain anonymous. In spite of the precautions taken by interviewers, some participants may have chosen not to discuss certain types of conflict situations.

Finally, this research stems from the experiences of a single university. This is a large Canadian university with a strong research focus. Another distinct feature of this university is that it had been involved in an intensive process of strategic transformation during the four years preceding the research. The extent to which restructuring issues were reflected in the participants' narratives may have been due to this process.

Findings

The original data analysis identified eighty-two distinct themes pertaining to the perceived sources of conflict. These themes converged into eight metathemes:

1. Structural issues—factors related to the physical and social organization of the university environment

2. Miscommunication—problems related to transmitting or receiving information

3. Harmful behaviors—ways in which one person mistreats another, whether intentionally or not

4. Interpersonal differences—disparate beliefs, values, norms, and behaviors between two or more people

5. Personal characteristics—factors particular to one of the individuals involved; for example, psychological problems

6. Negative history—instances where past relationships were problematic

7. Difficult issues—subject matter that is inherently contentious because it involves the evaluation of organizational members by their superiors

8. Emotions—feelings such as mistrust, embarrassment and humiliation, fear, jealousy, and anger

This article focuses on structural issues, because this was the most common source of conflict identified by research participants, as well as being the theme most likely to distinguish conflict at a university from conflict in other types of organizations. Examples of miscommunication or interpersonal differences, for instance, could have occurred just as easily in a for-profit corporation as in a university. Prior to conducting the research, the research team had not predicted structural issues to emerge so strongly as the most common source of conflict.

Structural issues refers to factors in the work environment, including policies, procedures, and the physical work environment. Overwhelmingly, respondents suggested that these structural issues contributed negatively to the creation of conflict and how it was handled. However, the relatively few instances where structures did contribute positively will also be described throughout this analysis.

The most prevalent structural sources of conflict identified by research participants included competition, hierarchy, stressful work environment, and changes in the structure of the university or units within it. All four groups noted competition, hierarchy, and bureaucratic limitations. Students were the one group that did not view changes in the structure as a source of conflict. Perhaps they were not as aware of the changes, given their relatively short stay at the university and their focus upon their studies. Some students noted that the university was not a big part of their life. They came for classes and went on their way, so they did not tend to be cognizant of conflicts that did not affect them directly.

Competition was a pervasive theme in the university experience. For students, competition meant competition for admission, grades, jobs, and scholarships, as well as the competitive nature of many class discussions. In the stories provided, competition led to stress and disillusionment rather than to the motivation to work harder. Professors and administrators also noted examples of student competitiveness, though some expressed the belief that the students rather than the structure of the university contributed to competitive conflicts.

Professors, administrators, and support staff members all told stories about the competitive nature of the hiring, merit, and promotion processes, both for teaching faculty members and for non-teaching faculty members. In some instances, the systems for annual appraisals, tenure, and promotion were specifically blamed for inciting jealousy, alienation, tension, and verbal abuse. One professor said, "We all navel-gaze and talk to ourselves and evaluate ourselves every year, and we go through this stupid exercise of comparing apples and oranges. And hundreds of person hours are put into dividing up a pie that in any case is not very big, and most people deserve a bigger slice than what they get."

For professors, competition over scarce resources also included fighting for teaching assistants and research funding.

Professors and administrators recognized the value of collaborating but expressed concerns that people were "not working in the same direction," and money issues tended to promote competition for resources. In spite of team rhetoric used by some administrators, professors specifically noted that they did not see themselves playing on the same team with other professors and administrators, particularly those from other academic units. A number of participants noted that competitiveness seemed to be inherent in the offices of the university that were designed to represent different constituencies—for example, the union that represented staff versus human resources, which was viewed to represent the administration. Similarly, participants identified tension between the student government, the faculty association, and the staff union to the extent that each group often saw the other as "the enemy." Governance by voting was also seen as a means of pushing people into factions.

Some competitiveness was attributed to financial issues. Lack of resources, dwindling resources, and inequitable division of resources were each seen as contributing to conflict in the university. In order to compete successfully, many people resorted to building and protecting their own "turf" or "fiefdoms."

For some participants, competition was viewed less as a structural issue than as a personality issue. Those participants believed that academia draws in people who are competitive by nature. Others noted that if academics are competitive, they have learned to be so in the competitive context of their own education, including the dissertation process. By definition, one strives in academe.

The competition theme in this research confirms Baldridge's findings (1971) at New York University, where fragmentation into interest groups and power struggles were found to be important contributors to the way conflict emerged. Some theorists might argue that competition might be more aptly classified as a consequence of conflict rather than as a primary source of conflict. In the present study, however, research participants labeled competition as a source of conflict rather than as a response to other sources. They saw competition as part of the fabric or social structure of the university.

The concept of *hierarchy* within the university is related to competition but it extends beyond it. All four groups of research participants provided instances where the hierarchical structure of the university acted as a source of conflict. One support staff member confirmed that students and professors disregard support staff members so much that they do not even consider them as being part of the hierarchy. Other staff members identified their subordinate position to administrators and professors but did not consider students to be specifically part of the organizational hierarchy. Degrees, titles, and tenure also reinforced the hierarchical structure of the university, contributing to feelings of powerlessness or inequity in the ways that conflicts were handled. One administrator made the troubling comment that the "the people with the Ph.D.s are the ruling class of the institution. Until you reach that level, you're black, you belong to a different group, and you have no rights."

Participants noted that the system gave more credence to degrees and positions than respect for individuals or for the abilities of those individuals. Various participants identified a similar "pecking order" in the institution. Some expressed concerns that they could not socialize with people from a different level of the hierarchy. Others noted that decisions were generally made top-down, with little consideration from those below in the hierarchy.

In a simple but compelling story of disregard for those perceived to be from the lower ranks, one support staff member noted that during a severe snowstorm, students, professors, and administrators were advised to go home. Staff members were told to remain at the university, as if they were second-class citizens. This type of treatment led to anger and resentment that affected how the staff members perceived and dealt with future conflicts with the administration.

The fact that participants saw the university as hierarchical was not surprising. One consequence of the hierarchy to which the researchers had not been previously attuned, however, was the extent to which this dynamic led to the avoidance of issues. Although the researchers had not specifically set out to explore this issue, avoidance was overwhelmingly the most common means of dealing with conflict identified by research participants. Participants who avoided conflict often attributed this to the hierarchy and their relative powerlessness to deal with conflict in a constructive manner with people higher up the ladder. Students avoided expressing concerns about professors rather than confront superiors about how they felt mistreated, staff members went home frustrated, and professors spoke of isolating themselves rather than confronting administrators about anything controversial. Participants often expressed fear of retribution for even raising issues.

Some participants noted that the university had confidential processes intended to allow for safer ways to provide feedback, pursue grievances, or appeal decisions (including grades, annual appraisals, and charges of harassment). Many participants expressed dissatisfaction with these processes for reasons that sometimes seem to contradict one another. Some participants saw confidentiality as a way to avoid accountability; that is, because the process was confidential, nobody could question the fairness or competence of the process. Others viewed confidentiality as a sham. They provided stories of leaked information, including inadvertent and intentional rumors. Concerns expressed by a student about a professor or by an employee about a superior could easily get back to the person who was the subject of the complaint, setting the complainant up for retribution or other abuses of power. Because the participants were describing instances where they avoided making complaints, many of their concerns about confidentiality were based on their perceptions or on stories they had heard rather than on direct experiences of breaches of confidentiality. In other instances, participants felt burned by the process in one instance and were determined to avoid making any complaints in the future.

Although hierarchy was a common theme, paradoxically, participants also suggested that lack of leadership and lack of accountability acted as sources of conflict. To some extent, this could be explained as personal characteristics of the existing leadership. Still, many people did not see the system of hierarchy as one that supported positive leadership and accountability. One of the primary concerns was that leadership did not deal with conflict issues and there were no mechanisms in place to compel leadership to do something about these issues.

In terms of *stressful work environment,* participants commented on ever-increasing demands, low salaries, high tuitions, and lack of institutional support. Certainly, not all stress was work- or university-related, as staff members and students in particular spoke of multiple sources of stress (for example, personal life issues and work off campus). Still, many participants related the occurrence of stress and their ability to manage it as being related to the university environment.

Illustrations of the impact of a stressful work environment included:

- Students who had difficulty making the transition from high school to university, where there were fewer structural supports and higher demands

- Staff members who had inadequate workspace and experienced lack of privacy

- Professors with multiple responsibilities in teaching, scholarship, and service, without sufficient time to focus or perform each task well

- Administrators who were faced with impossible tasks such as scheduling classes and carrying out their teaching responsibilities in a manner that would make all students and teaching faculty members happy

Lack of choice within the university environment was a common theme—for instance, students who had no choice about who they were working with on group projects or who they were living with in dorms (compare Clower and Goodwin, 1982), compulsory classes, staff members who had no choice about whom they worked with, and professors or administrators who could not escape dealing with people whom they did not like to work with.

One of the most powerful sentiments to come out of the research was the existence of a "toxic work environment." Although many participants spoke of the university as a primarily positive place to work, others suggested that their units or departments were negative places in which to work. Sometimes, this toxicity was related to competitiveness, petty infighting, and emotional baggage created during one conflict that carried on and took on a life of its own. As one professor noted, the effects of working in a toxic work environment can be devastating, both personally and professionally.

He noted that "it makes things here very impotent. Nothing gets done appropriately. If it's ignored long enough, people will go away. It just gets swept under the rug. This place is hard to manage collegially, anyway. You have to get people on the side because they have so much autonomy in terms of their job description. On the other hand, if you make decisions and it's not based on data, then you hope like hell that people will just, you know, . . . they write lots of nasty memos and then it goes away. The people remember."

Participants were aware of support systems at the university, such as human resources, counseling, union representation, and going up the hierarchy of decision makers. Still, many believed that the university did not have sufficient structures in place to deal with long-standing conflicts and resentments, so toxic work environments were tolerated.

In another paradox, *changes in the structure* of the university were also viewed as a source of conflict. Although many people expressed dissatisfaction with the current structures, attempts to change the structure were not necessarily viewed as positive. For some, the prospect of change caused concern, or even fear: What will happen to my job, will I even have a job, and who will I be forced to work with? For others, the conflict stemmed from the way in which change was approached. Although some participants lauded the university's strategic transformation initiative, others did not trust it. They did not believe that their input was being seriously considered, or they believed that the university had ulterior motives—for example, to centralize power or to simply cut costs without improving the system. Mistrustfulness and frustration with regard to change processes were sometimes related to past experiences with changes at the university, where participants believed that nothing substantial had changed. One professor complained, saying,

> God, if one more time I hear how we, . . . you know me, . . . or the people like me, can't handle change when we have been begging for it and are so tired of having someone come in and say they've changed something, now do it the new way, when it's clear that all they're doing is what they were doing, but with new jargon. Like new procedures. There has been no real difference, but at some level, either they're too stupid or they figure we're too stupid to notice that nothing has changed. And then they accuse us of being unimpressed because we can't handle change. And they'll run little seminars for us in terms of how we can handle this.

Conclusions

Universities have developed a variety of responses to dealing with conflict, ranging from grievance procedures for professors and staff members to mediation programs, to conflict resolution training, and to arbitration procedures. Given the range of sources of conflict identified in the present study, we need to reconsider the types of institutional supports that are being proposed and implemented to determine what types of supports might be most appropriate to build the capacity of the organization to deal more effectively with different types of conflict (Kolb and Silby, 1990).

The most pervasive sources of conflict found in this study were *structural issues*. In contrast, many of the conflict resolution strategies identified in the literature provide conflict responses to distinct incidences of conflict—for example, how a person who experiences sexual harassment can seek a remedy from the university or how a student dissatisfied with a grade can appeal it. If the primary issues are structural, then case-by-case methods of conflict resolution do not go to the root of the issue. Proactive rather than reactive responses are needed. Furthermore, sources of conflict must be dealt with at an organizational or community level rather than at an individual level. The following discussion presents an array of options meant to stimulate creativity and thinking about different ways of approaching these issues. Certainly, each institution (educational or otherwise) will need to conduct its own organizational research to help determine its best plan of action, given the fact that the nature of social conflict must be understood within the culture(s) and contexts in which it takes place (Bean, 1976).

The voices of the participants in this study suggest that university administrators and conflict consultants should focus their efforts on structural sources of conflict, such as competition, hierarchy, a stressful work environment, and changes in the structure of the university. In terms of competition, for example, universities must reassess which aspects of competition are necessary or productive and which aspects of competition are obsolete or counterproductive. If competition is meant to inspire professors and students to aspire higher and try harder, is it really working? That is not to say that all competition within a university must be eradicated. A merit and promotion system could be based on rewards for work units or departments rather than rewards for individuals. This would promote not only collaboration within work units and departments but also competition between them. The question is, could this competition be directed constructively toward the common goals of the university, or would it simply foster greater divisiveness?

In terms of alternatives to competition between students, there are many models of education that suggest that learning should be predicated on the individual needs of the learner rather than on competition between learners (Knowles, Holton, and Swanson, 1998). This model of adult learning is not so different from the interest-based approach in the conflict resolution model that encourages people to identify their interests and work toward solutions that satisfy these interests (Fisher, Ury, and Patton, 1997). Although some professors and departments have embraced the collaborative principles of the adult learning model, we have yet to see a large research-intensive university experiment with this model carried out institution-wide. Is this model naïve, too idealistic, or too expensive, or do universities fear such a radical change as being too big a risk?

The narratives of this study confirm what prior research has said about the organizational structures of universities. The problem is not simply that there is a hierarchy; all too often there are conflicting or ambiguous lines of authority, communication, and roles. Are universities simply too big and diverse to be managed as a single organization? We can either tinker with the systems as they are or we can think about radical change. Rather than operate under the guise of a single institution, for instance, universities could perhaps be reconceptualized as a federation of departments, institutes, and work units. Autonomy, common goals, and interdependence would have to be negotiated in a manner similar to state-to-state relations within an international context.

Bing and Dye (1992) argue that hierarchical systems can be effective in organizations like the military, but they are incompatible with the academic nature of a university, where the purpose is to "seek and send truth." If people in a hierarchical organization are trained to follow a chain of command, then hierarchy tends to restrict creativity, debate, criticism, and the open examination of ideas. Alternatively, a collegial model—including all constituents in a university—promotes an open exchange of ideas about values, processes, and content. The challenge in implementing a truly collegial model is in how to persuade those in the positions of power to take the perceived risks of sharing power.

Regarding stressful work environments, modifications that may seem minor could have an incredibly profound impact. Staff members who worked in open areas, for example, expressed a need for privacy, but building walls to create separate offices may be costly. However, there may be less expensive ways of providing for privacy—for example, designating at least one private work space per department for staff use for situations requiring privacy, allowing flexible work hours so that certain staff members would have the option of coming into the office during quiet times, or identifying underused areas of the university to use for additional staff offices. Once again, the principles of collaborative, problem-based conflict resolution (Fisher, Ury, and Patton, 1997) could be used to redress structural issues on campus.

Although research participants found problems within the university structure, changes to the university structure also acted as a source of conflict. Any process of structural change within a university must emphasize the building of trust, particularly in universities where many constituents perceive a negative relationship between administrators, professors, staff members, and students. Universities are fraught with mixed messages: hierarchy versus collegiality, academic freedom versus evaluation by peers or professors, and teaching versus research versus service as priorities of the university. Various consultants promote the use of visioning—long-term planning, or strategic transformation exercises every five or ten years. The turmoil and anxiety that these exercises create would be worthwhile if they produced the intended results. Research participants expressed concerns that five or ten years later the old issues would still not be resolved. Bureaucratic forces make radical change difficult.

Because the process of structural change is so important to obtaining buy-in of the relevant constituencies (Carter, 1999), those facilitating these processes could draw upon process-oriented conflict resolution models that empower participants and ensure that people feel heard in the process of determining structural change. The goal of the structural change process would not be to eliminate or resolve conflict but would instead engage the entire university in a dialogue based on principles of openness, respect, and acceptance of diversity. This would help build a culture within the university that could deal more effectively with conflict.

References

Baldridge, J. V. *Power and Conflict in the University.* New York: Wiley, 1971.
Bean, J. P. *The Use of Anthropological Field Methods as a Means for Conflict Resolution in Institutions of Higher Education.* Iowa City: University of Iowa Press, 1976. (ED 127 887)
Bing, R., and Dye, L. "The Danger of Hierarchical Decision Making: How a Model 'Effective' College President Alienated and Embittered a Campus." *Academe,* 1992, *78* (4), 16–19.

Carter, S. "The Importance of Party Buy-In in Designing Organizational Conflict Management Systems." *Mediation Quarterly,* 1999, *17,* 61–66.

Clower, J., and Goodwin, G. C. "A Theory of Organizational Behavior Applied to College Housing." *College Student Journal,* 1982, *16* (1), 73–76.

Douglas, J. M. "Conflict Resolution in the Academy." In S. A. Holton (ed.), *Mending the Cracks in the Ivory Tower: Strategies for Conflict Management in Higher Education.* Boston: Anker, 1998.

Fisher, R., Ury, W., and Patton, B. *Getting to Yes: Negotiating Agreement Without Giving In.* New York: Penguin, 1997.

Fitzgerald, L. F. *Sexual Harassment in Higher Education: Concepts and Issues.* Washington, D.C.: National Education Association, 1992.

Fuller, S. A. "Implementing University Sexual Harassment Policies: Conflicts and Contradictions." Unpublished manuscript, Rutgers University, 1996.

Harper, L. F., and Rifkind, L. J. "Competent Communication Strategies for Responding to Sexual Harassment in Colleges and Universities." *CUPA Journal,* 1992, *43* (2), 33–52.

Hartman, J. B. "Change and Conflict in the University." *Journal of Educational Thought,* 1977, *11* (1), 3–15.

Holton, S. A. (ed.). *Mending the Cracks in the Ivory Tower: Strategies for Conflict Management in Higher Education.* Boston: Anker, 1998.

Jameson, J. K. "Diffusion of a Campus Innovation: Integration of a New Student Dispute Resolution Center into University Culture." *Mediation Quarterly,* 1998, *16,* 129–146.

Knowles, M. S., Holton, E. F., and Swanson, R. A. *The Adult Learner: The Definitive Classic on Adult Education and Training.* Houston: Gulf, 1998.

Kolb, D., and Silbey, S. "Enhancing the Capacity of Organizations to Deal with Disputes." *Negotiation Journal,* 1990, *6* (4), 297–303.

Lewicki, R. "Teaching Negotiation and Dispute Resolution in Colleges of Business: The State of the Practice." *Negotiation Journal,* 1998, *13*(3), 253–269.

Ludeman, R. B. "The Formal Academic Grievance Process in Higher Education. A Survey of Current Practices." *NASPA Journal,* 1989, *26* (3), 235–240.

Mertens, D. M. *Research Methods in Education and Psychology: Integrating Diversity with Qualitative and Quantitative Approaches.* Thousand Oaks, Calif.: Sage, 1998.

Ostar, A. W. "Institutional Conflict." In S. Holton (ed.), *Conflict Management in Higher Education.* New Directions for Higher Education, no. 92. San Francisco: Jossey-Bass, 1995.

Rowe, M. P. "Helping People Help Themselves: An ADR Option for Interpersonal Conflict." *Negotiation Journal,* 1990a, *6* (3), 239–247.

Rowe, M. P. "People Who Feel Harassed Need a Complaint System with Both Formal and Informal Options." *Negotiation Journal,* 1990b, *6*(2), 161–172.

Sproule-Jones, L. "Managing Diverse Commitments: Equity Issues." Unpublished report, 1998.

Volpe, M., and Witherspoon, R. "Mediation and Cultural Diversity on College Campuses." *Mediation Quarterly,* 1992, *9* (4), 343–351.

Warters, W. C. *Mediation in the Campus Community: Designing and Managing Effective Programs.* San Francisco: Jossey-Bass, 2000.

Warters, W. C. *"Campus Conflict Resolution Resources."* [Available at http://www.campus-adr.org]. 2002.

Allan Edward Barsky is a professor in the School of Social Work at Florida Atlantic University in Boca Raton. He also practices family and community mediation. His book authorships include *Conflict Resolution for the Helping Professions, Interprofessional Practice with Diverse Populations,* and *Clinicians in Court.*

What Mediators Do with Words: Implementing Three Models of Rational Discussion in Dispute Mediation

SCOTT JACOBS

MARK AAKHUS

This study identifies three models of rationality that mediators employ in interpreting conflict situations and formulating the most sensible and appropriate way to proceed. These models, critical discussion, bargaining, and therapy articulate what mediators presume about the nature of conflict and the framework of activity required to manage the conflict. The models were developed through a close analysis of a corpus of forty-one mediation sessions. The analysis shows that the substance, direction, and outcome of mediation is shaped by the framework of activity implemented by the mediator. This can be seen by the way in which arguments are deflected and discouraged in bargaining and therapy models. These models suggest that mediation competence can be understood in terms of two issues: which model to implement when and how best to implement any model in a stream of discourse.

Ordinary people bring to mediation a commonsense vision that their dispute will be resolved through reasonable argumentation. They expect to receive justice through discussion (Merry and Silbey, 1984). They assume that the best way to proceed is by bringing in the facts of the matter, establishing who is in the right and who is in the wrong,

NOTE: *Earlier versions of this article were presented at the National Communication Association's annual convention and to the NCA/American Forensic Association's conference on Argumentation (Jacobs, 1989b; Jacobs, Aakhus, Aldrich, and Schultz, 1993).*

determining relevant evidence, and so on. This does not mean that they do any of these things particularly well. Indeed, if they come voluntarily, they expect that mediation should help in this respect.

Yet mediators typically do not encourage this type of dialogue or attempt to improve it. Instead, mediators usually show lack of interest in such matters, often actively discouraging argument or otherwise redirecting the discussion away from argument. So there is characteristic tension between the conduct of mediators and the conduct of disputants. Why is this? This is a puzzle we propose to address in this article.

The Carburetor Controversy

We can see this puzzle in the following example of a mediation session from community mediation.[1] The session is rather commonplace in terms of the problems disputants face, resolutions reached, and trajectories of mediation discussions.

The disputants are the owner of an automobile repair shop and a dissatisfied customer. Two mediators jointly mediate the session. The customer is complaining that his car still has the same problem as when he first brought it in, despite the work performed on the car by the shop owner's mechanics. The customer claims that he approved the work on the carburetor because the mechanic led him to believe that repair of the carburetor would fix the problem. The customer paid a total of $141 to the shop owner, which included a diagnostic fee of $21 and labor fee of $120. The customer wants a refund of the $120, because rebuilding the carburetor did not fix the problem. The shop owner claims that he should not have to refund the money. The shop owner contends that the $120 is proper payment for the work of rebuilding the carburetor, regardless of whether or not the problem with the car was fixed. He contends that because his mechanics spent several additional hours trying to diagnose the problem (about $120 worth), he has already undercharged the customer by charging only the minimum standard charge of $21 for the diagnosis. The shop owner further contends that no auto mechanic could guarantee in a case like this that the first set of repairs would solve the problem or that additional work might always be needed. The dispute is finally resolved when the customer and owner agree to a compromise settlement of a $60 refund. What is of interest here is how this compromise was achieved.

Throughout the mediation session, both the customer and the shop owner orient to the facts of the matter and to questions of fairness, justifiableness, and accuracy. For example, after the initial presentations and elaboration of their views of what happened, the customer responds to the shop owner with the following:

Excerpt One

60 DISSATISFIED CUSTOMER: As someone who's, who is relatively ignorant, relative to his expertise in a car, I am relatively ignorant as to the mechanics of a car. Therefore, I was relying on his expertise. He did not say, . . . as I recall, he did not say that he, that it might be in the carburetor, but he did not know what it was. He said they had . . . he said that they had, uh, limited it to the carburetor, that the message was . . . that I got was, that that was the only thing it could be, because everything else was OK. In fact, in fact, that is almost a quote. It's OK, up to the carburetor, so therefore it must be the carburetor. And I was relying on his expertise there.

61 MEDIATOR TWO: You've already told us what you think ought to be done to solve the problem. Uh, what do you think oughta be done, uh, Mr. O.?

62 OWNER OF AUTOMOBILE REPAIR SHOP: We invested roughly $120 worth of labor in this car before we . . . before we charged him to do the carburetor, which we were basically out of. Uh, there's $72 [worth of] labor charged on the job to rebuild the carburetor, uh, and at this point here, I don't feel that there's any adjustment needed. I think that there may be some additional repairs needed on the car. I don't feel that the work we done was . . . that [what] we did was uncalled for or out of line. If, uh, . . . if it had been taken to another shop, the same procedures and the same type of diagnosing repair procedure would have been done, uh, and I feel that we were very just in what we charged him for repairing the carburetor. Um, we were willing to take a loss on the first day's diagnosis, since nothing showed up and, uh, like I say, we let it go out the door that first day with just, with just the standard minimum charge of $21, and we've already invested a $120 before we, you know, we . . . like I said, we were willing to invest that much in a car to determine what it was and take a gamble, but once we found out that it had problems with the carburetor and we repaired that, uh, I think that we're well justified in what we charged and what, what we did on, um, billing for the repair work that was done on the car.

It is noteworthy in excerpt one that both disputants attempt to put forward and engage the arguments of the other disputant. The customer tries to establish the premise that it is reasonable to rely on the predictions and advice of experts. The shop owner tries to show that there is no certainty in assessing car troubles and that his shop did not take advantage of the customer's lack of expertise when they absorbed much of the cost of diagnosis.

The disputants use evidence and explicit reasoning aimed at constructing criteria for judging the claims of the other. The disputants continue to respond to the arguments made by each other during the mediation, as in excerpt two.

Excerpt Two

120 OWNER OF AUTOMOBILE REPAIR SHOP: We did the work. We did it properly. We . . . he was informed properly about the car, and if he has additional problems with the car, you know . . . I regret that he's got additional problems with the car, but it's not because we didn't do our job properly or [because] we overcharged or we built something wrong or we did the car . . . did something wrong with the car. It's because it's got a, a problem with the car that is a[n] intermittent problem, and it's very difficult and you have to do . . . it's, it's just like *doctors;* they call it exploratory and there's no, there's no questions about paying a bill for exploratories when you go into the doctor's to get something checked out. But when somebody comes to a mechanic, they say "I'm goin' to pay X number of dollars and I want this car to work properly and never have any problems after that," and you just can't do that when you're working on cars sometimes, and, and Mr. C. should have been aware of that from what we had discussed prior to this.

After one of the mediators suggests that the disputants split the difference, the customer in excerpt three addresses both the shop owner's argument and the justifiability of the settlement proposed by the mediator. The customer appeals to evidence and criteria to show that the mediator's suggested solution is not justified.

Excerpt Three

150 DISSATISFIED CUSTOMER: Well, like I said, have said before, I'll . . . me . . . I'm willing for him to either rebuild the carburetor or for him to pay me $60, and I don't feel like I . . . Heh, I feel like my original

position is fair, that, that he did not have the expertise. I think in, in many, many ways, he has said that, that it's extremely difficult . . . if, at least for him to, to analyze these type problems. He's said that repeatedly over and over again, which substantiates my position. He, he and I don't, I don't uh, impugn his, his general ability to repair cars. There, I'm an insurance agent and there are insurance matters which I have not, no, uh, ability to handle, uh, and I think that this is a particular case where he does not have the ability to handle the problem. That's what . . . my original position. And that's why he did not handle the problem—again, not otherwise impugning his, his ability. Uh, so I think my original position that he, he [should] refund me the whole $120 is, is fair. And then certainly, er, splitting—that is, you know, fair, and I paid him for the diagnosis. I paid him specifically the $21 for the diagnosis. Uh, I just feel like I'm being extremely fair with him, uh . . .

The disputants are clearly trying to reach a decision through a type of debate process; however, it is equally clear that the mediators are not interested in that type of process.[2] Notice in excerpt one that the second mediator actually turns away from the customer's arguments to ask for a proposed settlement from the shop owner. In excerpt three, the customer explicitly orients back to settling the differences, based on facts and values rather than simply splitting the difference.

Whenever the disputants pursue their disagreement by debating, the mediators attempt to change that way of interacting into something like bargaining. Excerpts four, five, and six illustrate the mediators' orientation toward pursuing the resolution of the disagreement. Early in the mediation, after hearing initial statements and discussion by the disputants, one mediator formulates over twenty minutes of debating in the following way.

Excerpt Four

35 MEDIATOR TWO: All right, then the only thing we need to be concerned about here is, uh, is the fact that he thinks that you should return a hundred and, uh, $20, and you think you shouldn't, right? Well, how can we get that solved? What would you be willing to do just to get this solved?

Later on, when the disputants lapse into further debate, the mediators cut off the arguments with the following:

Excerpt Five

135 MEDIATOR ONE: I think we've gone over all these facts.

136 MEDIATOR ONE: Yeah.

137 MEDIATOR TWO: Several times, and, uh, what we need to do is get a solution, if possible.

And again, when the disputants attempt to elaborate their reasons, the mediators press for a solution.

Excerpt Six

145 MEDIATOR ONE: Well, that doesn't help your solution here but [then] . . .

146 MEDIATOR TWO: [Well,] there's a, uh, a misunderstanding in communication here on both sides, I think, uh. . . . Mr. O, what do you think ought to be done to get this solved? Or do you think it's unsolvable?

Diagnosis

Even though the preceding excerpts do not present all the arguments made by the disputants or cleanly track the flow of the session, it should be clear that the disputants are arguing over who is justified and which proposal is fair. This does not mean, of course, that they have produced high-quality arguments, that they have fully explored the issues raised in their dispute, and so on. The mediators, on the other hand, generally restrict their contributions to straightforward clarification questions and to open-ended invitations for further comments. Then, once both sides have been laid out, the mediators begin pressing for proposals to solve the problem rather than encouraging further argument to resolve differences in the two accounts or to reconcile differences of opinion. The compromise settlement of $60, then, is not really based on a resolution of the disputants' arguments but rather results from a way of avoiding the need to come to such a resolution. So what is it that is going on?

One focus might be on the apparent bias or active encouragement of a particular solution. This is what Greatbatch and Dingwall (1989) call "selective facilitation." The general problem of mediator neutrality and impartiality or the lack thereof has been a general interest of mediation researchers (Cobb and Rifkin, 1991a, 1991b; Cohen, Dattner, and Luxemburg, 1999; Dingwall, 1988; Folger and Jones, 1994; Garcia, 1995; Greatbatch and Dingwall, 1989, 1999; Hale and Nix, 1997; Harrington and Merry, 1988; Jacobs, forthcoming, 1992; Kolb and Kressel, 1994; Rifkin, Millen, and Cobb, 1991; Tracey and Spradlin, 1994). This is an important topic, but its focus is on the substance of individual practice. As a result, it draws attention from the structuring of the activity format itself.

There is something else going on in the carburetor controversy that is not captured by the idea of selective facilitation. The mediators and the disputants have competing visions of the most rational way to proceed in handling the disagreement. The disputants pursue one vision, which is something like debate, whereas mediators pursue another vision, which is something like bargaining. There has not been a great deal of attention to the biases and structuring tendencies of the type of activity parties engage in, and there has been little discussion of alternative frameworks of activity. This is not a matter of individual bias but, rather, structural biases built into the activity type itself—if these are going to be called biases at all.

We shall argue in the following sections that mediators characteristically take in to mediation a model of rational discussion that might be dubbed bargaining, and sometimes they use other models. We have identified at least two others that are occasionally used. But the point to see in the preceding example is that the tension between the mediators and the disputants exists at the level of their different understandings about the most rational way to proceed in resolving the dispute. Prior mediation research supports the idea that there may be multiple rationalities through which mediators make judgments about how to intervene. Kolb (1983) distinguishes labor mediators as "orchestrators" who create the conditions for settlement or as "dealmakers" who lead the parties to settlement. Harrington and Merry (1988) identify three kinds of mediators, based on the different ideological "projects" in which they are engaged. They argue that mediators practice mediation to deliver dispute resolution services, to foster social transformation, or to foster personal growth and development in disputants. Kolb and Kressel (1994) distinguish mediators in terms of either a "settlement" stance committed to finding a substantive deal or a "communication" stance committed to helping disputants understand the problem, if not to settle it.

In a sense, the three models of rational discussion we will overview also exhibit themselves as different "styles," but the styles of mediating we see are ways of implementing deeper conceptions of the nature of conflict itself and are best understood as aspects of an effort to implement a system of activity that includes the disputants as well. These three models are not simply three different strategies of implementing rational discussion; they are three different conceptions of what rational discussion would be.

Three Models of Rational Discussion in Dispute Mediation

In this section, we illustrate and describe in more detail the three models of mediator rationality we have identified. We first describe our method of *normative pragmatics,* and then we discuss the three models of mediator rationality.

Normative Pragmatics

Our method follows the principles of normative pragmatics (van Eemeren, Grootendorst, Jacobs, and Jackson, 1993), where actual communication practice is described relative to a normative ideal of communication practice. The results can be used in two ways. First, everyday action can be judged relative to expectations of the normative ideal in order to cultivate better practices. Second, the normative ideals can be judged relative to our intuitions about the possibility and suitability of actual practice in order to promote better standards.

Discourse ideal. The analysis begins by selecting a plausible idealization of the discursive activity. In previously posing the puzzle of the carburetor controversy, we tacitly appealed to the model of *critical discussion,* developed by van Eemeren and Grootendorst (1984, 1992; van Eemeren, Grootendorst, Jacobs, and Jackson, 1993). Critical discussion is a communication activity in which disputants attempt to resolve their differences of opinion by putting forward arguments for and against their positions, testing the quality of those arguments, and coming to a mutual consensus of opinion based on the merits of the arguments made.

Following van Eemeren and Grootendorst (1992),[3] we can outline expectations for mediator contributions to a mediation. Mediator contributions should draw attention to forms of fallacious reasoning and prevent disputants from shifting the discussion toward other types of discussion, such as quarreling. Mediator contributions should draw out the argument potential in disputant messages so that the disputants can pursue the resolution of their conflict through reasoned discussion grounded in common values and acceptable evidence. If dispute mediators encouraged critical discussion to resolve differences of opinion, one would expect mediator messages to perform functions like the following:

- Determine the points at issue
- Recognize the positions that the parties adopt
- Identify the explicit and implicit arguments
- Analyze the argumentation structure
- Solicit evidence, reasoning, and counterarguments

Data. We assume that mediators make their interpretations and judgments in the flow of interaction, and that they are largely unaware of the details of this process. So rather than relying on interview or survey techniques to identify models of rationality, we have examined transcripts of mediation sessions. This type of data provides a more realistic picture of what mediators do than do practitioner stories and accounts of practice (although the latter are useful for understanding practitioners' native theories).

Three Models of Mediator Rationality

Mediators can be seen to work with at least three distinctive models of rational resolution of disputes. We have termed these three idealized models: critical discussion, bargaining, and therapeutic discussion. As Table 1 suggests, each of these three models is associated with a characteristic kind of communication activity that is based on a distinctive understanding of the nature of the conflict and the most rational way to proceed to resolve that conflict. While mediators do sometimes mix and move among these models within any session, we will treat these frameworks of rationality as distinctive ideal types, for purposes of exposition and because we have observed in our corpus of cases a dominant mediator style.

Critical discussion. As previously discussed, a *critical discussion model* of conflict resolution assumes that the source of conflict is a disagreement over facts and values that are public in nature. It is the public quality of the substance of a disagreement that both engages the disputants and provides the possibility for resolution. Disagreements engage disputants because they are based on assertions that lay claim to the belief of the person making the assertion *and* to the belief of those addressed. It is this public quality of an assertion that also provides an avenue for resolution by checking competing assertions for their consistency with public knowledge. So argument in critical discussion is not obstinate quarreling, cynical sophistry, or

Table 1. Models of Rationality

	Critical Discussion	Bargaining	Therapeutic Discussion
Source of Conflict	Disagreement over facts and public values	Conflict between competing wants and interests	Failures of mutual respect and mutual understanding
Optimal Solution	Claim that is most consistent with available facts and values	Proposal that maximizes gain and minimizes costs to both parties	Definition of the situation that acknowledges and affirms each party's point of view
Principle of Resolution	Public Justifiability	Mutual Acceptability	Sincerity and Openness
Process of Resolution	Argumentation and Refutation	Offers and Concessions	Self Disclosure, Explanations, and Definitions
Mode of Resolution	Agreement	Contract	Reciprocal Affirmation

self-serving adversarial debate. It is instead the joint construction of the best possible case, given the facts and shared values of the disputants.

On this model of conflict resolution, the optimal solution to a conflict is to determine that assertion which is most consistent with the available facts and values that constitute the common ground of the engaged parties. This amounts to a principle of public justifiability. Any assertion must be justified in terms of this common ground. And the process by which this is done involves the forwarding of arguments to support or refute the assertions in question. This model, then, assumes that disputants are able to produce and recognize good arguments, and that they are willing in principle to accede to the force of the better argument. The ultimate mode of resolution, if all works well, will be an act of agreement by both parties to some particular assertion that is based on their conviction that the asserted claim is correct.

Were mediators to work within the framework of critical discussion, they could be expected to intervene in ways that attempt to improve the quality of arguments and to guide the argumentation in more productive ways. As noted earlier, mediators tend not to do this. Of course, sometimes they do adopt something like a framework of critical discussion. The following excerpt contains one such attempt and also illustrates the problems mediators sometimes face in trying to use critical discussion as a means of resolving disagreements. This episode is taken from a mediation case in which a divorcing husband and wife are discussing visitation arrangements for their children. The husband wants more time with the children. The wife has agreed to allow him to see the children one day more each week (Tuesday), and the mediator has asked the wife whether her husband can pick up the children at school or at the house.

Excerpt Seven

01 WIFE: I really believe picking them up at the house is better, because that way there's more of the ongoing consistency after school with . . . You know, I'm going to have to get a sitter once I get working, anyway, so . . .

02 MODERATOR: Then [he'll] take them to school Wednesday morning?

03 WIFE: No, I'm not talking about overnights [pause] . . . I'm not talking about overnights. Our daughter is so incredibly emotionally upset right now [that] she won't even sleep unless she sleeps with me.

04 MODERATOR: Oh.

05 WIFE: She is upset about going with Ken right now. Yesterday I had to force her to go with him. I won't do that to those children.

06 HUSBAND: Kim? She does the same thing when she has to leave my apartment.

07 WIFE: OK.

08 HUSBAND: We've got the same situation. [pause]

09 MODERATOR: One of the problems, then, that I see here is that [pause] when they're with you, and you see one reaction, when they're with you, and you see another reaction, and . . . I gather that you find it inconceivable that they would say this at their father's house.

10 WIFE: No, I don't. No, I don't really. I haven't seen it. I can tell you that . . . [but I don't] find it inconceivable.

11 MODERATOR: [So you don't.] But because you haven't seen it, then you, ah [pause], ah, you find it difficult.

12 WIFE: Uh-huh.

13 MODERATOR: To, well, to, . . . to think that they would say that just to, ah . . .

14 WIFE: Huh? [No.]

15 MODERATOR: And he, on his part, can't see what they do over [there].

16 WIFE: [Oh,] he's seen it, he has seen it numerous times.

17 MODERATOR: [Oh, really?]

18 HUSBAND: Like what, Kim?

19 WIFE: Pardon me?

20 HUSBAND: Like what?

21 WIFE: Like last night, when she didn't want to go with you [and the other night when I sat in the living room . . . {with} her . . . to go].

22 HUSBAND: [I had the same thing last . . .]

23 WIFE: [With] you.

24 HUSBAND: [Night.] Kim, when she, we, . . . it was time to [leave].

25 WIFE: [OK.] What I'm saying is, I haven't seen it.

26 HUSBAND: I [know].

27 WIFE: [It's] conceivable. I haven't se[en any of it; you] have.

28 HUSBAND: [You ought to have.]

29 WIFE: Seen it. [You've] seen me have to carry her out to the car.

30 HUSBAND: [Yeah.]

31 WIFE: And [put] her in.

32 HUSBAND: [Yeah.] You haven't seen me have to carry her [from the apartment crying and yelling].

33 WIFE: [OK, I'm saying that that's right.] I have not seen it. I have not [ever] seen it.

34 MODERATOR: [And what] is true [is] that Kim had to, ah, encourage.

35 WIFE: Rachel.

36 MODERATOR: [Is] Rachel to go with you?

37 HUSBAND: Yeah, last night—the same way I have to encourage her.

38 MODERATOR: What was Rachel's reaction last night?

39 WIFE: She didn't want to go with him.

40 MODERATOR: She cried, or . . . ?

41 WIFE: She just hung onto me and said, "I don't want to go with daddy; I want to stay with you. I don't want to go with daddy."

42 MODERATOR: I see.

43 WIFE: And I said, "You'll have a good time when you get there and . . ."

44 HUSBAND: An' I have the same problem 'bout every other week, 'bout the same time Kim has, when it's time to leave the apartment. I had the same problem last night.

45 MODERATOR: Have you at any time gone to the apartment, say, [to see] the children?

46 WIFE: [Uh-huh.] [Oh,] not to pick them up, no. I've . . .

47 HUSBAND: [Right.]

48 WIFE: Gone to the apartment but not to pick them up.

49 MODERATOR: If you were to go and pick them up, do you think you would see this reaction in Rachel when she does not want to leave . . . Ken's house? [pause]

50 WIFE: That puts me in a difficult position, so, no, I don't think I would see that reaction, but it's a possibility.

51 MODERATOR: Uh-huh.

52 HUSBAND: That's why I think [that] if there wasn't this, you know, half a month between seeing the children and then only having them for two hours in the evening, ah, [we could] . . .

53 WIFE: [starts to interrupt]

54 HUSBAND: 'Scuse me. Could I finish, please?

55 WIFE: Uh-huh.

56 HUSBAND: It would mean a lot more ongoing frequent quality time and sharing of the children.

Notice that in this excerpt, despite the heated quality of the exchange between Kim and Ken, the line of argument is rather clear. Kim is saying that their daughter Rachel cannot stay overnight with Ken because Rachel is too emotionally distraught at this point to be away from her mother for that length of time. Her proof is that Rachel has to sleep in the same bed with her mother and becomes hysterical when she has to leave her mother and go with her father. Ken argues that this is not good proof that Rachel should not stay overnight, because on the days that Ken has Rachel she also becomes hysterical when she has to leave her father and go with her mother. Her hysteria is no special reason for the daughter to stay with the mother rather than with the father. And, presumably, Rachel's emotional distress is from the separation of the parents and would diminish if she had a more balanced time with both of them. Kim attacks Ken's argument by seeming to imply that Rachel does not really become hysterical when she has to leave her father.

These lines of argument are elaborated through the mediator's questions. Evidence is called out. And the implications of Kim's position are explored. And through his questioning, the mediator more or less challenges the legitimacy of Kim's defense (in turns 10, 25, 27, 33)—that is, that Ken has seen Rachel crying when she leaves for her father's, but Kim has not seen Rachel crying when she leaves to return to her mother's. This does not imply that Rachel does not do as Ken reports—a point that Kim finally more or less concedes in turn 50.

The problem that mediators commonly face in managing mediation as critical discussion is that where argumentation might appear needed to resolve a disagreement, the arguments advanced by one party rarely lead to concessions by the other party. Where a value is advanced by one party in defense of a position, it is often deflected by a counterbalancing value advanced by the other party (Jacobs, 1989b). Or where one party assembles facts to justify a proposal, those facts may not be accepted by the other party. And where mediators do intervene to critically examine the basis for a position, disputants may simply be unwilling to accept the force of the conclusion. They may shift to new grounds for their position or they may shift back to previously dropped positions (see discussion of the lines of questioning by mediators in chapter six of van Eemeren, Grootendorst, Jacobs, and Jackson, 1993). Worse yet, where arguments are made by disputants, they are sometimes used to establish blame and censure, initiating a counterproductive spiral of attack and defensive counterattacks that leaves the parties further from resolution than when they began (Jacobs and Jackson, 1992; Jacobs, Jackson, Stearns, and Hall, 1991).

These problems of trying to gain assent to the force of the better argument or even to establish any claim with certainty are illustrated in the preceding excerpt. Notice that Kim's concession in turn 50 is equivocal at best. And her phrasing unwittingly reveals an all too common obstacle: a reluctance to admit to the force of an argument when it leads to an unwelcome conclusion. What, exactly, is the "difficult position" that Kim is put into? And how does being put into that difficult position lead to her conclusion that she doesn't think she would see Rachel crying when leaving Ken's apartment? The only difficult position Kim seems to be in is the position of having to admit that her refusal to let Ken have Rachel overnight doesn't have any firm grounds. But notice also that there is no evidence for believing that Rachel also cries when she leaves her father's apartment other than by Ken's report. And the veracity of Ken's story is clearly something that Kim doubts. Finally, while the argumentation in this episode does not fully deteriorate into an irreparable exchange of hostilities, the potential was clearly present (compare with similar episodes discussed in Jacobs and Jackson, 1992; and Jacobs, Jackson, Stearns and Hall, 1991).

In any case, the encouragement of a more critical discussion is not a common response by mediators to the arguments of disputants. And when it is pursued in this way, that pursuit is limited and local.

Bargaining. A *bargaining model* of conflict resolution assumes that the basis for conflict is not so much a disagreement over facts and values as it is a conflict of interests. The conflict is over not what the parties believe but, rather, what they want. Whereas the critical discussion model finds disputants unable to come to a common representation of the world, the bargaining model finds them unable to arrive at a joint plan to achieve individually desired ends. Given this conceptualization of the problem, resolution will be achieved by locating those plans that improve the standing of both parties relative to the status quo. This domain of plans constitutes a "zone of agreement" within which a solution to the conflict is to be found.

The optimal solution will be to find within this zone of agreement that solution which maximizes the gain and minimizes the cost to both parties. This solution assumes a principle of mutual acceptability—that the solution is to be arrived at by accommodating the self-interests of both parties. And the way in which this optimally satisfying proposal is reached is through a process of offers, counteroffers, and concessions as the parties locate conditions of acceptability for the other party and narrow down the options.

As we have noted before, both the critical discussion model and the therapeutic model play only marginal and subordinate roles in most mediation sessions. The dominant framework for conflict resolution by the mediators we have observed is something like a bargaining model. Within the kind of activity called for by this conception of conflict and its resolution, arguments are interpreted mainly in terms of the canonical act, types of bargaining. They are seen as implicit proposals, concessions, or rejections of proposals. In this way, arguments are seen in terms of what the disputants want and are willing or unwilling to concede. Within the framework of a bargaining model, considerations of fact and value are contained within the boundaries of what each party is willing to offer or accept. This is often evident in the initial stages of mediation after disputants are asked to present their sides of the complaint or to explain why they are in mediation. Mediators will frequently ask for proposals or they will summarize disputant arguments in terms of what they want or are willing to concede.

Within a bargaining framework, mediators tend to interpret arguments as attempts to resist proposals rather than as attempts to reason together. Rather than finding in the back and forth of argument and counterargument an opportunity for resolving disagreement, mediators usually see evidence of entrenched resistance and an unwillingness to accommodate to the other party. This is the way the mediators in the carburetor controversy managed the mediation. It is also characteristic of how the mediator in the following excerpts manages the dispute.

The following three excerpts are taken from a divorce custody case in which the husband (Carl) is asking for a return to something like a previously shared custody arrangement, whereas the wife (Natalie) wants to keep the current arrangement where she has sole custody and the husband has weekend visitation rights. Both Carl and Natalie seem intent on justifying their positions in terms of which arrangement will work, which arrangement is fair, and whether the other is taking positions in good faith. But, like the case of the carburetor controversy, the mediator in this session seems generally uninterested in exploring these issues and responds to arguments with calls for suggestions and questions of what each party is willing to accept.

Excerpt Eight

01 HUSBAND: I mean, we had them together. We['ve] raised them together so far. Just because she's mad at me is no reason to take them away from me.

02 WIFE: Well, I'm not trying to take them away from him. [I . . . the arrangement . . .]

03 MODERATOR: [Could you . . . Could] you go along with the, uh, shared raising part of the arrangement? As Carl . . . as he was suggesting?

04 WIFE: Uh, week to week I don't know, because I don't know how that's going to work out. I don't think it would work out as well as, um . . .

05 MODERATOR: That would be a joint arrangement—a joint physical arrangement where you both would have, uh, equal time, equal responsibility, equal time off, if you wanna call it that, uh, and you both would have an equal opportunity to . . . to be an influence on the children's life.

06 WIFE: OK, well, he, uh, . . . I don't think that would, uh, . . . I wouldn't agree to that.

07 MODERATOR: If you don't, the [court will].

08 WIFE: [But see,] even though he says that, um, the weekends, um, he doesn't get equal time. Well, he works on the weekends and I work during the week. Also, during the time that I am supposed to have them . . . and it's not, . . . there is . . . It seems to me that if he wants . . . OK, he . . .

09 MODERATOR: Make a suggestion, then. I hear what you're saying. I hear what you're saying. Make a suggestion, then. What do you think Carl doesn't like about the [every other weekend]?

10 WIFE: [OK, I don't] know what, uh, his off days are, but it seems to me that if he were a manager writing his own schedule . . . And he says that we couldn't arrange it [with the other off days].

11 MODERATOR: [Keep it. OK.] Natalie, give us a choice or give us an idea [of] what . . . How can we resolve this?

12 WIFE: Uh, OK. What kind of arrangement?

13 MODERATOR: Uh-huh.

14 WIFE: Um, OK. If he doesn't wanna agree to just keeping them on the weekends, then . . . uh, let's see. Maybe Wednesday, Thursday, [and] Friday we'll both work. Well, you would have . . .

Excerpt Nine

47 MODERATOR: OK, but you're saying [that] you could live with that?

48 HUSBAND: Yeah.

49 MODERATOR: Saturday to Tuesday.

50 HUSBAND: Exactly Saturday to one . . . yeah, to Tuesday.

51 MODERATOR: Natalie, uh, would you go along with that, too?

52 WIFE: Uh, no, I'd rather [have] the full custody.

53 MODERATOR: Why is it . . . ? [Why don't you] want him to have any custody of the children?

54 WIFE: [Because . . . uh . . .]

55 HUSBAND: 'Cause she wants to hurt me.

56 WIFE: No, I . . . OK, . . . no, I'm not trying to hold this against you, I'm not. I don't hate you, I'm not trying to keep them away from you. Um, if we could arrange something that . . . If you know that . . . OK, since you're in charge of [your] department . . . If you know that you're gonna have regularly, um, . . . Tuesday, Tuesday and Wednesday off, or Tuesday and Sunday off, see . . . Because a lot of times, he'll say that, um, he's gonna keep them . . . Sunday, Monday, and Tuesday on that arrangement, and then he will be working on that day [or he won't].

57 MODERATOR: Excuse me, Natalie. Excuse me, Natalie. What, what are you saying? What is the bottom line to what you're saying?

58 WIFE: OK.

59 MODERATOR: Be more specific with me, would you please?

60 WIFE: I would like full custody of the children because I feel like with Robert's condition . . .

61 MODERATOR: OK, I understand that. Before, it was working out OK.

62 WIFE: No, it was[n't].

63 MODERATOR: [It] wasn't [working out], [OK]?

64 WIFE: [No, it wasn't] working out [with them], where I kept them Wednesday, Thursday, and Friday, and he kept [them] . . .

65 HUSBAND: [It wasn't] working out?

66 WIFE: No, because we would end up arguing and fighting and um . . .

Excerpt Ten

85 WIFE: Well, if you knew if we were gonna have this arrangement where[by] you kept them [on] Sunday, Monday, and Tuesday, and I kept them [on] Wednesday, Thursday, and Friday and [on] alternate Saturdays, then it'd seem like we would, should, both know our schedules [for the week], but see a lot of times I don't.

86 HUSBAND: [But see that . . .]

87 WIFE: Know[ing] what time he was going to work, uh, who was going to pick up the kids, whether he was going to pick them up or not or, um, whether he was going to leave them in child care or not, what his arrangement was, . . . because a lot of times we were in the . . .

88 MODERATOR: So, what you're saying is, you don't mind Carl [having] . . . [sharing, OK?]

89 WIFE: [I don't] mind sharing them with [him, but] we need some kind of definite schedule, um, worked out better than it [was].

The mediator's main concern in these excerpts seems to be what Carl "could live with" and what Natalie "would go along with"; see turn 09 of excerpt eight. See also turns 47 and 51 of excerpt nine. Suggestions and concessions, not arguments, seem to be what he is looking for. When the mediator calls on Natalie to "be more specific," in turn 59 of excerpt nine, he is calling for a more specific proposal, not more specific evidence or argument. And the questioning in turns 53, 63, and 65 of excerpt nine come off more as challenges to make concessions than as calls for justification or clarification. This is all characteristic of a bargaining orientation.

Notice also the persistent response of the mediator to arguments. Excerpt eight begins with Carl and Natalie arguing over whether or not Natalie's position is fair and well intentioned. The mediator, in turn 03, cuts it off with a question as to whether Natalie will "go along with the, uh, shared raising part" of Carl's suggested arrangement. In turn 09, he cuts off the wife's argument with "make a suggestion" and again, in turn 11, he tells her to "give us a choice." In turn 57 of excerpt nine, the mediator again cuts off Natalie's argument and calls for "the bottom line to what you're saying." When the wife begins making an argument, in turn 60, again the mediator cuts it off. When the mediator says, "I hear what you're saying," in turn 09 of excerpt eight, and "I understand that," in turn 61 of excerpt nine, one gets the impression that what he hears and understands are contributions that do not "give us an idea [of] how can we resolve this" dispute (turn 11).

Excerpt ten contains an especially telling move. Notice how the mediator's response in turn 88 maps the wife's contributions onto the geography of a zone of agreement. Natalie has again lapsed back into arguing why Carl's proposal will not work and why it is not a better solution to their problems than the current arrangement. The mediator's summary statement in turn 88 does more than simply clarify the substance and force of her objections; it actively transforms their nature. Not only does the summary shift the valence of the remarks from negative to positive; it also casts the objections into information about the nature of the zone of agreement within which a resolution might be had. The wife is drawn into a commitment to sharing the children as long as a definite schedule might be had. (Discussion of a similar case can be found in example 6.1 of van Eemeren, Grootendorst, Jacobs, and Jackson, 1993, chapter six.)

Therapeutic discussion. A *therapeutic model* of conflict resolution assumes that the conflict in question arises from a misunderstanding of the other party's point of view or failure to respect the rights of the other party to hold his or her point of view. On this model, disagreements and conflicts of interest are only apparent, or they are really only symptoms or fronts that would dissolve if deeper relational conflicts were articulated and addressed. Within a therapeutic framework, resolution of the conflict will be achieved when the disputants recognize and accept each other's point of view.

The optimal solution will be to arrive at a definition of the situation in which each party's identity claims can be validated and interpreted in ways that do not impinge on the claims of the other. Like Goffman's notion (1959) of a "working consensus," what is sought is not so much an agreement on substantive matters as a modus vivendi in which each party is defined in a way that is granted respect and tolerance. Such a consensus assumes (contra Goffman) twin principles of sincerity and openness. A genuinely workable relationship must be built on the willingness and ability of each party to articulate and disclose his or her true feelings and point of view and the readiness to empathically understand and accept the other party's disclosures. As with Katriel and Philipsen's discussion (1981) of the "communication" concept in American culture, the therapeutic model holds that resolution is achieved through a process of "talking through" problems in a way that is both disclosive and supportive. This process assumes a kind of interpretive rationality, an imaginative capacity to construe situations in multiple ways so as to arrive at an interpretation that also encompasses the feelings and experiences of the other parties. When mediators do try to give shape to the messages advanced by the disputants by employing strategies that are consistent with a therapeutic conceptualization of conflict, messages tend not to be treated as assertions aimed at resolving a difference of opinion in their own right but are, instead, treated as expressions symptomatic of underlying frustrations and unresolved emotions.

One characteristic strategy of therapeutic mediators is to treat messages not as *assertives* that lay claim to the beliefs of all parties but, rather, as *expressives* that must be acknowledged and affirmed. For example, the following exchange occurs in a divorce custody session in which the husband and wife are trying to decide who should get the children the morning of Easter Sunday. After the husband has said that he would take them for the morning, the wife becomes quite agitated and complains that the husband also had the children on Thanksgiving Day, and that he had "railroaded" her into having the children for Christmas Day with his relatives over to her house, and she concludes by exclaiming, "I really think this is unfair. *I just do! I'm sorry.*" When the husband starts to refute her claims (saying that he had the children for only half of Thanksgiving Day and that she was the one who invited his parents over), the mediator cuts him off:

Excerpt Eleven

01 HUSBAND: I'm just, you know . . . [If she could see those things.] [OK.]

02 MODERATOR: Wait, [I'm] . . . I think Jane is just expressing a feeling, [whether] the details are true or [not].

03 HUSBAND: [OK.]

04 MODERATOR: Not. She's just [expressing] a feeling.

05 HUSBAND: [OK.] Yeah, OK, that's a good point: feelings versus details. Thank you.

06 MODERATOR: And I think if you try to point out the times and dates, [it wouldn't] get us anywhere. It's just a feeling that she's expressing.

By this sort of strategy, mediators defuse utterances of argumentative force. Attitudes and feelings sincerely expressed may be legitimate and should be respected, even if what is said may not be true. In this regard, a therapeutic mediator shares with a bargaining mediator what may appear to be indifference to "the facts." It is not at all uncommon for mediators to say things like, "It's not a matter of who's right or wrong or good or bad or moral or immoral or any of those things; I don't care."

In similar ways, mediators may cut short debates by attributing their disagreement to a "misunderstanding" or a "communication problem." Or they may try to portray arguments as reflecting the fact that each party has a different point of view on the situation. By transforming the force of the arguments in this way, each party's arguments are relativized, and the conflicts are seemingly dissolved, or at least the arguments are disqualified as viable grounds for either party's position.

Therapeutic mediators may also address the entire argumentative exchange at a metalevel and treat the arguments as symptomatic of deeper relational dysfunctions (for example, Moderator: "OK, at some point now, you've gotta work some things out in a different way perhaps"), they may treat them as expressions of deep-seated feelings that need to be overcome in an effort to take the other party's point of view (for example, Moderator: "Well, Mr. Johnson, if those things occurred, I imagine you know I can understand your being very angry at her, but she still wants to be close to her children, and your moving to Alaska really removes the children from her, so you can understand her hurt about that").

But it is especially characteristic of the therapeutic model to actively probe for feelings and attitudes that might seem irrelevant within a bargaining model or a critical discussion model. Feelings and attitudes that stand as obstacles to reconciliation must be articulated and resolved. Excerpts twelve and thirteen come from a dispute between neighbors over a barking dog. Becky has brought a complaint against her neighbors, Luke and Cathy. Notice how the second mediator seems to be concerned with issues that do not readily fit the concerns of a critical discussion or bargaining definition of the sources of conflict.

Excerpt Twelve

117 LUKE: I . . . I'll acknowledge that, uh, our guys were making some noise. Uh, we . . . we've spent some time and attention with them and, as you say, it's . . . it's gotten much better. Um, if it's not completely better at this point, it certainly is improved. Uh, what has not been improved is things that are still around the neighborhood, which, uh, are making as much noise as ever. So I'm wondering how we happened to get more of your attention?

118 BECKY: Because it's so close.

119 LUKE: Uh, what . . . ?

120 MODERATOR ONE: Can you identify what . . . what works, as far as working with the dogs? Can you tell us what's working?

121 LUKE: Um, we've . . . we've just . . . Just tell 'em no or bring 'em. We'll bring 'em back in the house, . . . yeah.

122 MODERATOR TWO: Cathy, you . . . you . . . When you started talking about this, part of me feels that we should just say, "Oh, look at the dog issue." But it sounds like you have some hurt feelings that may be affected by how you feel about this dog issue. Are there some of those that you want to share without you[r] know[ing] taking it completely away from the dog issue? For some of this may be important, um, for us to know, for everyone here to hear how you feel.

123 CATHY: I don't know if that's relevant. I mean, she all but said she doesn't like us. And I felt, what else can be said?

124 MODERATOR ONE: I didn't hear that.

125 CATHY: You didn't hear that? She made an issue not to get to know us or to say anything to us. That means she doesn't want nothing to do with us, not even to say hello.

126 MODERATOR ONE: Looks like you're the hurt . . . Your [feelings] . . .

127 CATHY: [Not to speak] . . . Turn your head when you see somebody . . . You won't acknowledge [them]?

128 MODERATOR ONE: [I'm] going to ask you to keep your voice down. Cause, . . . let's try to . . . You know . . . Work it out and [try not] to make anybody wrong.

129 CATHY: So, I mean, that's obvious . . . that I just want to solve the dog issue.

130 MODERATOR ONE: Well, sometimes.

131 CATHY: And forget the rest.

132 MODERATOR TWO: Sometimes, you have to consider if there [are] some other feelings that you have that this is an opportunity to say some of those things and maybe understand each other better.

Excerpt Thirteen

151 MODERATOR TWO: Are there some other things that you could [mention that] maybe we should know?

152 LUKE: I would like to say, uh, that, uh, at this point, we have stopped feeding those birds. I don't know if that is still an issue with you, but, uh, we've cut that out.

153 MODERATOR TWO: How do you feel about doing that? Stopping?

154 LUKE: [Not good] at all. I think it is an infringement.

In turn 122, the mediator invites one of the complainees (Cathy) to talk about potentially hurt feelings, thus opening up the broader issue of relations between the neighbors. While Cathy doubts the relevance of this, both mediators push the issue, actively encouraging the kind of expressions of feeling that most mediators ignore or try to discourage. In turn 132, the second mediator then frames this broader topic as an "opportunity" to "maybe understand each other better."

Likewise, in turn 151 of excerpt thirteen, the second mediator again takes the opportunity to encourage fuller communication between the neighbors. And when Luke reports that he has also stopped feeding the birds (Becky had complained that the birds came into her yard and made a mess), the second moderator does not respond by asking Becky if the problem has been stopped (as would be expected in a bargaining or critical discussion model). Instead, the second moderator asks Luke how he feels about doing that. Again, the focus is on encouraging more open communication and on resolving the kind of emotional and relational problems that are taken to be the real source of current and future conflicts.

Conclusion

The issue of mediator competence should involve (1) the ability to choose which model to apply to any particular session and to any particular moment in the session and (2) the skills with which a mediator implements any particular model. In the end, a competent mediator may be the one who has mastered the three models of rationality articulated here, or possibly only one, but the competent mediator is always judicious about how, when, and where any particular model is put into play.

Notes

1. Transcribed excerpts of mediation sessions are drawn from a corpus of forty-one mediation sessions (each around one hour in length), from three different mediation agencies in western and southwestern American cities. Only the face-to-face interactions between the mediator(s) and both disputants were recorded. The cases involve nineteen child custody/visitation disputes referred to mediation by divorce courts, with the remainder of the cases consisting of customer complaints, neighbor disputes, tenant/landlord conflicts, and the like, mediated by neighborhood dispute resolution agencies. See Donohue (1991) and Pearson and Thoennes (1984) for further description of the transcripts and the mediation center involving the custody/visitation disputes.

2. The dominant sense of argument that researchers seem to focus on is that of aggravated quarrelling (for example, Garcia, 1991; Greatbatch and Dingwall, 1997) rather than the kind of arguments we see in the carburetor controversy case. Greatbatch and Dingwall (1997) have pointed out that disputants sometimes exit from this kind of argument on their own. However, they also point out that these arguments rarely end in agreement. The problem mediators face in managing critical discussion is directing arguments to a constructive resolution and conclusion that all can accept.

3. In the terminology of speech act theory (van Eemeren and Grootendorst, 1992; Searle, 1976), the would-be arguments of disputants are treated by mediators not as a type of justifying representative but as motivated expressives that are symptomatic of underlying frustrations and unresolved emotions. Representatives are acts that assert propositions and they can be either true or false. Expressives are acts that avow attitudes and feelings and they can only be sincere or insincere. The clearest cases are acts like saying "Thanks," which express gratitude, or exclamations like "Wow!" which express pleasant surprise.

References

Cobb, S., and Rifkin, J. "Neutrality as a Discursive Practice: The Construction and Transformation of Narrative in Community Mediation." In S. Silbey and A. Sarat (eds.), *Law, Politics, and Society.* Vol. 11. Greenwich, Conn.: JAI Press, 1991a.

Cobb, S., and Rifkin, J. "Practice and Paradox: Deconstructing Neutrality in Mediation." *Law and Social Inquiry,* 1991b, *16,* 35–62.

Cohen, O., Dattner, N., and Luxemburg, A. "The Limits of the Mediator's Neutrality." *Mediation Quarterly,* 1999, *16,* 341–348, 1999.

Dingwall, R. "Empowerment or Enforcement? Some Questions About Power and Control in Divorce Mediation." In R. Dingwall and J. Eekelaar (eds.), *Divorce Mediation and the Legal Process.* Oxford: Clarendon Press, 1988.

Donohue, W. *Communication, Marital Dispute and Divorce Mediation.* Hillsdale, N.J.: Erlbaum, 1991.

Folger, J., and Jones, T. "Epilogue: Toward Furthering Dialogue Between Researchers and Practitioners." In J. P. Folger and T. S. Jones (eds.), *New Directions in Mediation: Communication Research and Perspectives.* Thousand Oaks, Calif.: Sage, 1994.

Garcia, A. "Dispute Resolution Without Disputing: How the Interactional Organization of Mediation Hearings Minimizes Argument." *American Sociological Review,* 1991, *56,* 818–835.

Garcia, A. "The Problematics of Representation in Community Mediation Hearings: Implications for Mediation Practice." *Journal of Sociology and Social Welfare,* 1995, *22,* 23–46.

Goffman, E. *The Presentation of Self in Everyday Life.* New York: Anchor Books, 1959.

Greatbatch, D., and Dingwall, R. "Selective Facilitation: Some Preliminary Observations on a Strategy Used by Divorce Mediators." *Law and Society Review,* 1989, *23,* 613–641.

Greatbatch, D., and Dingwall, R. "Argumentative Talk in Divorce Mediation Sessions." *American Sociological Review,* 1997, *62,* 151–170.

Greatbatch, D., and Dingwall, R. "Professional Neutralism in Family Mediation." In S. Sarangi and C. Roberts (eds.), *Talk, Work and Institutional Order: Discourse in Medical, Mediation and Management Settings.* Berlin, Germany: Mouton de Gruyter, 1999.

Hale, C., and Nix, C. "Achieving Neutrality and Impartiality: The Ultimate Communication Challenge for Peer Mediation." *Mediation Quarterly,* 1997, *14,* 337–352.

Harrington, C., and Merry, S. "Ideological Production: The Making of Community Mediation." *Law and Society Review,* 1988, *22* (4), 709–735.

Jacobs, S. "Speech Acts and Arguments." *Argumentation,* 1989a, *3,* 23–43.

Jacobs, S. "Finding Common Ground and Zones of Agreement: Two Models of Rationality for Conflict Resolution." In B. Gronbeck (ed.), *Spheres of Argument: Proceedings of the Sixth SCA/AFA Conference on Argumentation.* Annandale, Va.: Speech Communication Association, 1989b.

Jacobs, S. "Argumentation Without Advocacy: Strategies for Case-Building by Dispute Mediators." In F. H. van Eemeren, R. Grootendorst, J. A. Blair, and C. A. Willard (eds.), *Argumentation Illuminated.* Dordrecht, the Netherlands: Stichting International Centrum voor de Studie van Argumentatie en Tallbeheersing (International Society for the Study of Argumentation), 1992.

Jacobs, S. "Maintaining Neutrality in Dispute Mediation: Managing Disagreement While Managing Not to Disagree." *Journal of Pragmatics,* forthcoming.

Jacobs, S., Aakhus, M., Aldrich, A., and Schultz, N. "The Functions of Argumentation in Models of Conflict Resolution." Paper presented at the Speech Communication Association of America annual convention, Miami, Fla., Nov. 1993.

Jacobs, S., and Jackson, S. "Relevance and Digressions in Argumentative Discussion: A Pragmatic Approach." *Argumentation,* 1992, *6,* 161–172.

Jacobs, S., Jackson, S., Stearns, S., and Hall, B. "Digressions in Argumentative Discourse: Multiple Goals, Standing Concerns, and Implicatures." In K. Tracey (ed.), *Understanding Face-to-Face Interaction.* Hillsdale, N.J.: Erlbaum, 1991.

Jefferson, G. "Discourse Transcription." In J. Maxwell Atkinson and John Heritage (eds.), *Structures of Social Action: Studies in Conversational Analysis.* Cambridge, U.K.: Cambridge University Press, 1984.

Katriel, T., and Philipsen, G. "'What We Need Is Communication': 'Communication' as a Cultural Category in Some American Speech." *Communication Monographs,* 1981, *48,* 301–317.

Kolb, D. *The Mediators.* Cambridge, Mass.: MIT Press, 1983.

Kolb, D., and Kressel, K. "The Realities of Making Talk Work." In D. Kolb and Associates (eds.), *When Talk Works: Profiles of Mediators.* San Francisco: Jossey-Bass, 1994.

Merry, S., and Silbey, S. "What Do Plaintiffs Want? Reexamining the Concept of Dispute." *Justice System Journal,* 1984, *9,* 151–178.

Pearson, J., and Thoennes, N. "A Preliminary Portrait of Client Reactions to Three Court Mediation Programs." In J. A. Lemmon (ed.), *Reaching Effective Agreements.* San Francisco: Jossey-Bass, 1984.

Rifkin, J., Millen, J., and Cobb, S. "Toward a New Discourse for Mediation: A Critique of Neutrality." *Mediation Quarterly,* 1991, *9,* 151–164.

Searle, J. "The Classification of Illocutionary Acts." *Language and Society,* 1976, *5,* 1–24.

Tracey, K., and Spradlin, A. "Talking Like a Mediator: Conversational Moves of Experienced Divorce Mediators." In J. P. Folger and T. S. Jones (eds.), *New Directions in Mediation.* Thousand Oaks, Calif.: Sage, 1994.

van Eemeren, F., and Grootendorst, R. *Speech Acts in Argumentative Discussions.* Dordrecht, Cinnaminson: Foris/Berlin: Mouton de Gruyter, 1984.

van Eemeren, F., and Grootendorst, R. *Argumentation, Communication, and Fallacies: A Pragma-Dialectical Perspective.* Hillsdale, N.J.: Erlbaum, 1992.

van Eemeren, F. H., Grootendorst, R., Jacobs, S., and Jackson, S. *Reconstructing Argumentative Discourse.* Tuscaloosa, Ala.: University of Alabama Press, 1993.

Scott Jacobs is a professor of communication at the University of Arizona. His research focuses on discourse pragmatics and conversational interaction, argumentation, and dispute mediation.

Mark Aakhus is an assistant professor of communication at the School of Communication, Information, and Library Studies at Rutgers University in New Brunswick, New Jersey. He examines the role of human and machine mediation of learning, organizing, decision making, and conflicts/disputes.

Disputing Neutrality: A Case Study of a Bias Complaint During Mediation

ANGELA CORA GARCIA
KRISTIE VISE
STEPHEN PAUL WHITAKER

Researchers find that some participants in mediation hearings report that the mediator was unfair or biased, but disputants rarely communicate these perceptions to the mediator, and very rarely do they do so during the mediation hearing itself. During data collection for a study of mediation hearings, a videotape of a small-claims mediation hearing was made in which a disputant did make such an accusation during the hearing. This serendipitous capture of an accusation of bias on videotape enables us to examine how a mediator's actions during the hearing may have contributed to a disputant's perception of unfairness. Narrative analysis is used to show how mediation techniques such as empowerment, representation of disputant positions, story summarizing, and emotion work can cause a perception of bias if they are applied unequally.

Although most disputants report satisfaction with the mediation process (Bahr, 1981; Depner, Cannata, and Simon, 1992; Kelly, 1989; Kelly and Duryee, 1992; Parker, 1980; Pearson and Thoennes, 1985; Waldron and others, 1984; Benjamin and Irving, 1995), some disputants do report perceptions of mediator unfairness or bias (Chandler, 1990; Gaughan, 1982; Gaybrick and Bryner, 1981; Kelly, 1989; Meierding, 1993; Irving and Benjamin, 1992; Saposnek, Hamburg, Delano, and

NOTE: *The Law and Social Sciences Program of the National Science Foundation provided funding for the data collection (grant SBR-9411224). The C. P. Taft Memorial Fund at the University of Cincinnati also contributed to the support of this project. We would like to thank the mediator and disputants for allowing their hearing to be videotaped, and we also wish to thank the anonymous reviewers, whose feedback greatly improved this article.*

Michaelson, 1984; Benjamin, 1995). However, these perceptions are rarely expressed during the hearing itself. Most previous research on mediator bias is based on survey or interview data. Although these methods are useful, they cannot directly examine the process of creating a perception of bias. An interactional analysis of an actual mediation hearing is needed to explore how an impression of bias or nonneutrality can be created.

During data collection for a study of mediation hearings, a videotape of a small-claims mediation hearing was made in which a disputant made an accusation of bias during the hearing. This serendipitous capture of an accusation of bias on videotape enables us to examine what aspects of the hearing may have led to the bias complaint. Our goal in this article is to determine what went wrong in this hearing. What sequence of actions led to the disputant's bias complaint, and what was the role of the mediator in this process? Answering these questions will show some ways in which mediators can avoid creating perceptions of bias.

Data and Methods

The mediation hearing analyzed in this article was one of thirty mediation sessions videotaped for a study of the creation of agreement in mediation hearings. The videotape was transcribed using the techniques of conversation analysis (Atkinson and Heritage, 1984; see transcribing conventions in the exhibit). The mediator in this hearing is an experienced, professional mediator, and, as she stated during the hearing, this was the first time she had been accused of nonneutrality. At the time that these data were collected, she had been working for several years at a city-run mediation center in the Midwest.

First, we describe the hearing and the emergence of the bias complaint. We then describe the potential triggers of the bias complaint, such as how the mediator used empowerment, story solicits, representation of disputants' positions, summaries of disputants' stories, and emotion work. We conclude with a discussion of the implications of our analysis.

Description of the Hearing and the Emergence of the Bias Complaint

The hearing begins with a brief description of the mediation process by the mediator, followed by her request to hear the complaint of the plaintiff (Sheila). Sheila describes the relationship between herself and the defendant (Doreen) as a casual, work-related one. She claims that she lent a compact disc (CD) player and $250 to Doreen and that Doreen failed to return these items. She offers as "proof" an audiotape that allegedly captures a telephone conversation she had with Doreen's boyfriend (Andrew), during which the boyfriend states that they still have the CD player. Although Sheila offers to play the tape, the mediator initially says that it is not necessary for her to hear it. As Sheila completes her story, the moderator makes a point of telling her that she will have a chance to respond to anything Doreen might say.

When it is Doreen's turn to respond, she frames her "story" as a denial of Sheila's accusations by asserting that she had not borrowed $250 from Sheila and that she does not have her CD player. Instead, Doreen insists that Sheila's claims are motivated by a desire to maintain contact with her. She describes their friendship as one she maintained out of "pity" because, she claims, Sheila had no other friends. Furthermore, she cites Sheila's alleged involvement in illegal activities and her history of violent behavior as reasons for her wanting to terminate the relationship with Sheila. Doreen also states that Sheila frequently tapes telephone conversations, thus suggesting that the use of the audiotape would be proof that Sheila's claims are problematic.

After Doreen tells her version of the story, the moderator asks for Sheila's response. Sheila first addresses the "facts" of Doreen's argument, and then she turns her attention to the more "emotional" parts of Doreen's story. The moderator's questions focus primarily on the emotional aspects of the case (how this has affected Sheila, how it has hurt their friendship, and so on), and she reminds Sheila and Doreen that the goal of mediation is to "work something out that satisfies both of you." She tells them that in the courtroom only "the proof" counts, "not your feelings, not your emotions, nothing but the proof."

The mediator then asks Sheila for proof of her claims. Sheila has no documents supporting her claim that the loan was made, but again she offers as evidence the taped telephone conversation between her and Doreen's boyfriend, Andrew. This time, the moderator tells her that she is welcome to play the tape. Doreen again objects to the tape being used as evidence and accuses the moderator of being biased against her. She states that the moderator expressed concern for Sheila's level of stress several times without offering her similar support ("And I hear you say, 'Oh, this must be stressful on you, this must be stressful on you.' Why is it that you feel that it's just oh so stressful for Sheila?"). The mediator disagrees with this challenge to her neutrality ("Doreen, I'm really sorry if it seems to you like I am playing favorites, because I'm actually not"). Doreen responds by reformulating and reissuing her complaint about the mediator's unequal response to their stress levels ("But you did say that to her a few times. Why do [you] feel that she may be under so much stress and I'm not?"). When the mediator denies feeling this way, Doreen asks, "Well, why is it that you brought it out to her and not to me?" Then, the moderator responds argumentatively ("Why did I use every word in the English language that I used with you and I probably did not use every word in the English language that I used with her?") and reiterates her claim that she is not taking sides ("I'm really sorry that you feel like there needs to be sides here, because there's not. You know? I'm just doing my job. I'm not on one side or another"). This response apparently does not appease Doreen, because she interrupts the moderator's final sentence to elaborate her complaint ("But I did hear you state that twice to her . . . and you said you're not worried about emotions here, but that was asking [about] her emotions. Is that not true?"). Jennifer again defends herself ("I don't think that I did say I wasn't worried about emotions. I think emotions are very important. And how you feel is just as important. I believe I gave you ample time to talk. I asked you at least twice if you had anything else you wanted to say"). Doreen uses the claim that she was given sufficient time to talk as a jumping off point for her second main complaint ("But then you went back to Sheila again, which gave her two times to talk"). The exchange continues in an argumentative fashion. The moderator decides to end the hearing because of the accusation of unfairness.

While the mediator's response to the bias complaint is not the focus of this article (we are concerned with *why* the bias complaint occurred), it is interesting to consider how a different response might have rescued the situation and restored disputant confidence in the mediator and the mediation process. The mediator made several attempts to placate Doreen after she made her accusation of bias, and to tell her that she was mistaken—for example, "I'm really sorry if it seems to you like I am playing favorites, because I'm actually not. I'm really sorry that you feel like there needs to be sides here, because there's not. You know? I'm just doing my job. I'm not on one side or another." But the mediator's attempts to placate Doreen fall flat because she does not provide evidence to support her claim that she is not biased. Perhaps the mediator's disclaimers would have been more persuasive if she had explained why she did what she did—for example, why she was concerned with Sheila's stress levels, and why she was asking Sheila about her feelings. The main problem, however, seems to be that at times the mediator slips into an argumentative mode as she discusses the bias complaint with Doreen. Perhaps she could have announced a "time out" from the mediation to discuss the bias complaint calmly, or she could have called a caucus to talk with Doreen privately about the bias complaint so that she could have explained more openly why she treated Doreen and Sheila the way she did.

It should be emphasized that it is our research question that caused the disputant to feel that the mediator was biased, not whether the mediator was in fact biased or not. What is important for mediation practice is to learn more about how a mediator's actions affect perceptions of the disputants, so that mediators can act in ways that will present an impression of fairness and impartiality. If a disputant perceives bias, we want to know why, so that we can avoid such situations in the future.

Potential Triggers of the Bias Complaint

In this section we will discuss how the mediator's actions could have contributed to Doreen's perception of bias. Are there ways she could have employed mediation techniques differently, in order to avoid the perception of asymmetrical treatment that emerged? There are a few actions that could be identified as possible mediator "mistakes." For example, the mediator may not have described the mediation process and her role in it thoroughly enough at the beginning of the hearing. When the mediator opens the hearing, she does not tell the disputants that they can have multiple chances to tell their stories. Later in the hearing, Doreen assumes that she has only one chance to tell her story, whereas Sheila has two chances. But most of the problems in the hearing seem to emerge as a result of applying standard mediation techniques (such as empowerment, story solicits, intervention in or responses to disputant's stories, or emotion work) unequally or without sufficient sensitivity to how each disputant perceives the mediator's interaction with the other. The interactional problem, from the point of view of the mediator, is how to play to two audiences simultaneously.

Empowerment

Empowerment is one of the ways mediators can ensure that mediation is a fair process when (as is usually the case) the disputants are unequal in power, status, or knowledge (Neumann, 1992). As Barsky (1996) notes, one view of empowerment is as a method of power balancing. The mediator identifies the weaker party and helps him or her compensate for these inequalities (see also Harrington, 1985; Regehr, 1994; Wall, 1981; Tjosvold and Van de Vliert, 1994).

As others have argued, this empowerment of one party raises practical and ethical issues (Matz, 1994; Regehr, 1994; Rifkin, Millen, and Cobb, 1991; Roehl and Cook, 1989). In particular, "if the mediator acts in a way that redistributes power, then the parties may see this as evidence of mediator bias against the more powerful party" (Barsky, 1996, p. 112). However, "if the mediator does not act to redress power imbalances, then the mediation process may be perceived as unfair" (Barsky, 1996, p. 112; see also Susskind, 1981; Stulberg, 1981). Empowerment is typically something the mediator does without announcing that he or she is doing it. Thus extra help or attention given to the "weaker" party may not be perceived by the "stronger" disputant as a legitimate difference in treatment, thus leading the party receiving less attention to believe that the mediator is biased against him or her. This is what may have happened in the hearing under consideration.

The "undercover" nature of the empowerment technique is also problematic because it does not involve the disputants in decisions about how the process will work. When mediators open hearings, they typically tell the disputants how the hearings will be structured. If they are not informed about the possible use of empowerment techniques, then they have not been adequately informed. This puts power in the hands of the mediator, which probably should be in the hands of the disputants. It is also possible that if the mediator makes independent decisions about who needs what kind of help without informing the disputants, any bias or partiality he or she may feel toward one of the disputants may be reinforced by this implicit alignment with one of them. Because the disputants will not know that empowerment is being used, they will not be able to protest against its use if they disagree with it or correct any errors in understanding that result from it. On the other hand, a mediator might say, "I will try to assist Disputant A because she has a problem communicating that will make it difficult for her to participate in mediation." Disputant B might respond by saying, "That's fine." Or he might say, "But I also have a problem communicating that I need your help with." The mediator might then get information that would enable her or him to understand more clearly the needs of both parties and may therefore be able to more accurately assess who needs what kind of help.

In the case being analyzed here, there is some evidence that the mediator may have perceived one disputant to be less competent than the other and therefore will have taken steps to empower her. By "less competent," we are not referring to their competence as persons or members of society; we are referring solely to their ability to participate in the mediation hearing. The mediator may have perceived Sheila to be less competent, involved, and cooperative than Doreen because the behavior of the two disputants differs greatly at the beginning of the hearing. Doreen gives the impression of a polite, attentive, calm, and cooperative interactant. She is seated, gazing at the mediator, and giving nonverbal responses at appropriate points in the mediator's speech. Sheila, however, is fiddling with her clothes and possessions, moving around, and avoiding eye contact. She does not appear to be attending to the mediator's remarks. This type of behavior, particularly at the hearing's onset, could signal to the mediator that Sheila will require extra care and attention to involve her in the mediation process. Thus, a pattern where Sheila gets more mediator attention and displays of concern than Doreen is established.

Second, when Sheila does begin to speak (in response to the mediator's solicitation of her story), her voice is monotonal and she speaks with unusually even rhythms; she sounds mechanical and distant. To the extent that Sheila's voice and speaking style make her sound less than competent, the mediator could be led to give her extra attention and accommodation.

During Sheila's account, the mediator takes several steps that appear to be attempts to empower her. These attempts become problematic later on in the hearing when Doreen shows that she perceived them as giving Sheila unfair advantages. In this particular hearing, the mediator's use of empowerment techniques might have been more successful if she had first checked out her perceptions of Doreen's competence before using empowerment techniques for Sheila (if she had interacted with both disputants a little at the beginning of the hearing, she might have come to a different assessment of the relative competence and needs of the two disputants). Second, the mediator failed to "play to two audiences"; while concentrating on empowering Sheila, she neglected to consider the effect of her actions on Doreen. Third, while perfect symmetry of treatment (as explained in the introduction) is not possible or desirable, there were several instances throughout the hearing where greater symmetry in her treatment of the disputants might have helped. We will now examine in detail the mediator's treatment of the two disputants in the hearing as it relates to the bias complaint.

Solicitation of the Disputants' Stories

The standard way mediation hearings are organized may interface with the empowerment issues previously described to create potential sources of asymmetrical treatment. Cobb and Rifkin's study (1991) of community-based mediation hearings shows that while there is a rhetoric of neutrality among mediation practitioners and advocates, the nature of the mediation process militates against actual neutrality. The first storyteller in the mediation hearing uses that opportunity to set the moral stage for the hearing—characterizing their own position as right and good and that of the opposing disputant as wrong and bad. Mediators unwittingly aid in the process of reaffirming the "primary narrative" by orienting to the issues raised by the first story as they facilitate the hearing. Unless mediators successfully aid the second disputant in promoting an "alternative narrative" that challenges the moral framework established by the primary narrative, they have failed in their goal of constructing the mediation hearing as a "neutral" process (Cobb and Rifkin, 1991).

The way the mediator solicits Sheila's story and Doreen's story supports Cobb and Rifkin's findings. The mediator's initial solicitation of Sheila's story was the question "What's been going on?" When the mediator solicits Doreen's story, her story solicitation is not parallel to the one she gave Sheila. The mediator's solicitation of Doreen's story is, "Why don't we give Doreen a chance to respond to some of the things that you've said? And also tell us what happened as she sees it." This makes it sound as if Doreen must first defend herself against Sheila's complaints. Compared with how Sheila's story was solicited, the solicitation of Doreen's story conveys skepticism (with the words "as she sees it"). The mediator's attempt to empower Sheila is shown by the care she takes to avoid giving the impression that Doreen's story will be given more credibility than Sheila's. Furthermore, the mediator's use of "we" and "us" in her solicitation of Doreen's story apparently refers to Sheila and the mediator. Because Doreen is mentioned by name and the mediator is looking at Sheila during this statement, the mediator thus aligns with Sheila in a way that excludes Doreen.

In general, the problem Cobb and Rifkin identify would be difficult to avoid without changing the format of mediation. There are two things the mediator could have done that might have helped. First, perhaps she could have begun the body of the hearing by having each disputant make a brief initial statement so that each party would have at least one chance to speak before either tells her "long" story. This structure would allow both disputants to respond to each other in their long stories rather than just the disputant who goes second. Second, the mediator might have tailored the words and phrases used to avoid privileging the first disputant's story or appearing to align with the first speaker. For example, avoiding "we" and "us" to align a mediator with one client against another, avoiding skepticism markers ("as she sees it"), and, in general, avoiding framing the second disputant's story as a "response" to the first disputant might all have lessened the likelihood of the perception of bias. In the case we're examining, the mediator's solicitation of Doreen's story ("Why don't we give Doreen a chance to respond to some of the things that you've said, and also tell us what happened as she sees it?") could have been replaced with the statement "Thank you for telling me what happened. Now, it is Doreen's turn to tell me what happened. Then you each will have a chance to respond to the other's statement." This version treats the two stories as equivalent in terms of their truth value.

The Mediator's Interventions in Sheila's Story

The mediator's actions during the disputants' stories are quite different. Her interventions in Sheila's story are supportive and facilitative, whereas her interventions in Doreen's story are generally challenging. As soon as Sheila begins telling her story, the mediator intervenes by asking for relevant details and helping Sheila produce the information she needs to understand what happened.

Excerpt One

SHEILA: I know Doreen because I work with Doreen at Parker's Restaurant.

MODERATOR: OK.

SHEILA: OK, we've been friends for, I guess, two years maybe?

MODERATOR: Were you [good] friends?

SHEILA: Well, I wouldn't say real good friends, you know. We . . .

MODERATOR: Did you see each other outside of work?

SHEILA: Uh, once in a while, . . . yeah, you know?

MODERATOR: OK.

SHEILA: Not a lot.

MODERATOR: OK. What's happened?

SHEILA: Uh, what has happened is, uh . . .

The initial hesitations and uncertainty markers in Sheila's story give the impression that she is having trouble getting her story launched—for example, the pauses and the use of "I guess" and "maybe." The mediator uses continuers (see Sacks, Schegloff, and Jefferson, 1974) such as "OK" and questions such as "Were you good friends?" "Did you see each other outside of work?" and "What's happened?" to help Sheila get her story off the ground.

The mediator continues to provide supportive responses throughout Sheila's story. At one point, Sheila deviates from the central issues. As Sheila gives unnecessary details, the mediator redirects her to the essential points by asking, "So what happened?" This question gets Sheila back on track. In sum, the mediator's frequent interventions in Sheila's story are supportive and consist mainly of continuers, supportive questions, and redirects intended to focus her story on the essential points. These are typical aspects of mediation work.

The Mediator's Interventions in Doreen's Story

The mediator does not offer Doreen the same type of help in storytelling that she gave Sheila. During most of Doreen's story, the mediator speaks little (perhaps because Doreen's fast, fluid speaking style does not convey a need for assistance). Although the mediator does provide some continuers, most of her interventions in Doreen's story challenge rather than provide support.

The first question the mediator asks Doreen occurs quite late in her story—after Doreen provides several reasons why she had no need to borrow money from Sheila. The mediator summarizes Doreen's denial that there was a loan and draws an upshot from it: "So you're saying there was no two hundred and fifty dollars?" Restating or summarizing is a routine part of mediation work, and it is often quite helpful in showing both disputants the import of a disputant's story, as well as helping the storytelling disputant to focus on the main points (Ury, 1993). However, the mediator's use of a skepticism marker (Whalen and Zimmerman, 1990) in this utterance ("So you're saying . . .") conveys doubt about Doreen's claims. Mellinger's research (1989) on emergency telephone calls shows that call takers who were skeptical of a call signaled this by writing "caller states" or "caller claims" in their computer report of the incident. The mediator's tone of voice as she produces this utterance sounds skeptical.

In addition, the questions the mediator poses to Doreen do not merely refocus the story, they challenge Doreen's story from the perspective of

Sheila's story (see Cobb and Rifkin, 1991). This type of mediator intervention, "replacing the disputant" (Garcia, 1995), occurs when the mediator actually assumes the role of one disputant to the other. "When 'replacing' the disputant, the mediator does not restrict him or herself to representing the disputant's expressed position[;] he or she goes beyond what the disputant said and argues in place of him or her" (p. 35).

In excerpt two, Doreen argues that the letters Sheila sent her show that Sheila is obsessed with her. The mediator first asks an informational question ("What kind of letters?"), but she uses a skeptical tone of voice. When Doreen's response indicates that she only received one letter rather than several ("The one that she has right here that she says she sent"), the mediator asks her to confirm whether that was the only letter received ("Is that the only letter?"). The mediator's informational questions work to deflate Doreen's initial claim that she had received a number of letters; thus Doreen's attempt to use the letter(s) as evidence supporting her claim of Sheila's obsession falls flat.

The mediator's intervention in this exchange becomes even less supportive of Doreen when the she sanctions Doreen for interrupting. Donohue (1989) finds that a struggle for control of the floor can escalate a mediator's emotional involvement in the dispute and can "distance mediators from formulating refined interpretations of disputant communication patterns" (p. 340). When this sanction occurred, Doreen was elaborating a reply to the mediator's prior question, so the mediator was actually interrupting Doreen rather than Doreen interrupting the mediator. However, the mediator says, "Let me finish." Once she has secured control of the floor, the mediator asks, "So you think that she's doing this two hundred and fifty dollar thing and the CD player thing simply to get reinvolved in your life?" Again, this utterance is not simply a summary of Doreen's position; the mediator is conveying skepticism of Doreen's claims by using the phrase "so you think" and the word "simply." When Doreen replies, "Yes, exactly!" the mediator again conveys skepticism by immediately countering with the question "How would that happen?"—in a skeptical tone of voice, thus suggesting that it is unlikely that it would happen.

Excerpt Two

MODERATOR: Tell me why you think Sheila says anything about the two hundred and [fifty dollars or the] CD.

DOREEN: [Because she wants . . .]

MODERATOR: Player?

DOREEN: Because she thinks that this is a way of getting back in[to] my life. She sent me letters . . . I totally ignored [them].

MODERATOR: What kind of letters?

DOREEN: The one that she has right here that she says she [sent].

MODERATOR: [Is] that the only letter?

DOREEN: That's the only letter! [And] I didn't get invo[lved bec]ause I didn't want to [call her].

MODERATOR: [So. Let me] finish. So you think that she's doing this two hundred and fifty dollar thing and the CD player thing simply to get reinvolved in [your life?]

DOREEN: [Yes!] Exact[ly!]

MODERATOR: [How?] How would that happen?

DOREEN: It won't! I . . . no matter what! And no matter what, even if I, . . . You know, I said the worse that can happen is that you can believe Sheila, what she says, and her little tape recorder, because she has hundreds of them!

MODERATOR: I'[ve got a very, very] easy job. I don't have to . . .

DOREEN: [But the point is . . .]

MODERATOR: Believe or disbelieve anybody. OK?

The mediator is responding to Doreen's story from the perspective of Sheila's story (Garcia, 1995). The questions the mediator asks Doreen during the opening of her story are directly related to the accusations Sheila has already produced. Doreen could perceive this as an attempt to squelch her position by forcing her to simply respond to Sheila's accusations (Cobb and Rifkin, 1991). However, in contrast to the mediator's questions to Sheila, which we saw as "helping" Sheila explain her story in detail, the questions asked of Doreen appear "accusing" in nature and seem to force Doreen to refocus her story to directly answer Sheila's accusations.

For example, in excerpt three, the mediator asks, "When's the last time she lent the CD player to you?" After Doreen answers this question, the mediator challenges Doreen by reminding her of the evidence that Sheila has brought with her: "Sheila says she has something on a tape!" Doreen responds by vigorously contesting the validity of the tape.

Excerpt Three

MODERATOR: When's the last time she lent the CD player to you?

DOREEN: Oh, it's been months! Well, in August, when we went to Georgia, I took . . . we took my sister's CD player, so it was way before then!

MODERATOR: Sheila says she has something on a tape!

DOREEN: Of Andrew! Well, it doesn't. When was this? If she'd lent me . . . ?

MODERATOR: I don't know.

DOREEN: [I'm.] OK. If she has a tape, how . . . for what day? When is . . . when could this be? If she [had] lent [me] the . . .

MODERATOR: [I don't.]

DOREEN: CD player numerous times . . . That tape could be from any of those times that she . . .

The techniques the mediator used to help Sheila tell her story are absent in her exchange with Doreen. Rather than provide supportive questions aimed at refocusing, she tends to use Sheila's story to challenge Doreen's account. The accusing and/or skeptical nature of her interventions could also have contributed to Doreen's perceptions of bias.

There are several issues that need to be considered here. First, neutrality and fairness in mediation do not necessarily mean treating each disputant exactly the same. The disputants do not present the same content, attitude, or interactional issues to the disputant, so identical, "script-like" responses would be ineffective. For example, as previously mentioned, Sheila's hesitancy in getting the story off the ground may require a different type of response or assistance from the mediator than Doreen's fluency. The trick is to provide what assistance is needed while making it clear that each is being given what is needed and no more. Perhaps the mediator could explicitly share her strategies and the reasons for them with the disputants. For example, she could say, "I will ask questions or otherwise intervene in your stories, as necessary, so that I can understand them, so that we can stay on topic, and so that I can help you get your statement out clearly. I may have to treat you differently at times in order to give each of you the help you need. Please do not be disturbed if I ask you different questions than I asked the other."

Second, mediators should be alert to the risk of being drawn in by the logic of the first story (Cobb and Rifkin, 1991). Mediators might want to avoid using the first story to critique the second as well as to avoid "repre-senting" the disputant (Garcia, 1995) or using skepticism markers (Mellinger, 1989). Mediators may find it helpful to have a separate question and answer session after each story is told to make such critiques, and, ideally, the disputants will make them, not the mediator.

The Mediator's Response to Each Disputant's Story

The way the mediator summarizes and responds to the disputants' stories could have also contributed to the bias complaint.

The mediator's summaries of the disputant's stories. As each disputant completes her story, the mediator summarizes and restates it. The mediator's summary of Sheila's story (excerpt four) is basically supportive of her claims.

Excerpt Four

MODERATOR: Let me see if I understand what you're telling me so far. You made a loan to her of two hundred and fifty dollars? With the understanding that Andrew would pay you fifty dollars a week?

SHEILA: That's what she was telling [me.]

MODERATOR: OK. That's what she was telling you. Nothing's been paid on that?

SHEILA: That's correct . . .

MODERATOR: And then you allowed her to use your CD player and you haven't seen your CD player since?

SHEILA: No, I haven't!

MODERATOR: OK. So, basically, that's it? You haven't seen the two hundred and fifty dollars? Or your CD player?

SHEILA: That's correct.

MODERATOR: Do you have any receipts for your CD player?

SHEILA: I purchased the CD player down in Atlanta, Georgia, last year.

The mediator's summary of Sheila's story—"You haven't seen the two hundred and fifty dollars or your CD player?"—is followed immediately by the question "Do you have any receipts for your CD player?" By moving directly from the story summary to requesting a document that could establish the value of the CD player, the mediator may give the impression that she is accepting Sheila's story as true without letting Doreen tell her side. Because Doreen has never denied the existence of the CD player, the mediator's question can be heard as trying to establish its value.

When the mediator sums up Doreen's story (excerpt five), she again says, "So you're saying," which may subtly convey skepticism. The mediator overlaps Doreen's denial with a continuer ("OK"), and then she immediately gives Sheila a chance to respond. Thus the mediator, in her effort to keep the hearing moving and to quickly get back to Sheila, prevents Doreen from producing her denial of the accusation in the "clear." Her lack of response (other than "OK") may make Doreen feel that the mediator is not listening to her.

Excerpt Five

MODERATOR: So you're saying that you're a very honest person [and that] you do not have two hundred and fifty dollars of hers and you do not [have her CD player]. Is that . . . ?

DOREEN: [I do not!] I do [not!]

MODERATOR: [OK.] Let's give Sheila a chance to respond to some of the things that you've said.

The mediator's completeness queries. As each disputant comes to the end of her story, the mediator responds with "completeness queries" (to make sure the disputant is done before moving on). The mediator's completeness queries differ for the two disputants. Sheila is given a wider latitude to add new material to her story than Doreen is (perhaps because the mediator is still striving to empower Sheila, the apparently weaker disputant). This difference between the mediator's response to the two stories may contribute to Doreen's perception of bias.

After Sheila has completed her story, the mediator asks her if she has anything she wants to add: "What I'd like to do now is give Doreen a chance to talk, unless you have something else you want to add." Sheila takes advantage of this invitation to produce a letter supporting one of her claims. The mediator then asks her a second time if she would like to add anything: "OK, anything else?"

When Doreen's story is complete, she receives a different type of invitation to speak from that which Sheila had received. The mediator asks,

"Is there anything new that you want to tell me right now, before we give Sheila a chance to respond?" The mediator's specification of "new" information is likely to be heard by Doreen as a strong limitation, because earlier in the hearing Doreen had been sanctioned for repeating herself.

Later on, the mediator gives Doreen a second chance to add to her story, but again this invitation is limited to showing more evidence. However, the mediator does not ask whether Doreen has anything else she wants to tell her. After Doreen says that she has no more documents to show, Doreen volunteers that she has more to say. She describes what she wants from the mediation. Instead of acknowledging or responding to this request/complaint (as the mediator did with the issues Sheila had brought up at the end of her story), the mediator interrupts Doreen and says, "Well, let's see what we can accomplish here" and then solicits Sheila's response. The mediator does not allow Doreen to elaborate or add to her story.

Excerpt Six

MODERATOR: OK. Is there anything else before we get with Sheila, that you wanted to show me?

DOREEN: No.

MODERATOR: OK.

DOREEN: But I do want to tell you [that] I'm still not angry with Sheila. I just want a separation! I just want my life—away from hers, and . . .

MODERATOR: Well, let's see what we can accomplish here, OK? Sheila, [why don't] you respond to some of the things she['s] said?

SHEILA: OK. First of all, . . .

In sum, the mediator's completeness queries constrain and direct Doreen's account but provide an opportunity for Sheila to elaborate her account.

Emotion Work

It is a common and legitimate mediator move to verbalize a disputant's expressed emotions to get them to acknowledge their feelings—a technique that might enable them to move beyond them (Ury, 1993). By bringing emotions to the fore, the mediator may also be trying to create a bond of sympathy between the disputants (Thoennes and Pearson, 1985) or to get them both to connect with their friendship for each other. However, in this hearing the mediator's attention to Sheila's emotions contributed to Doreen's perception of mediator bias.

According to Doreen, the mediator's statement to Sheila—"Some of these things must have been difficult for you to hear"—was one of the triggers for her bias accusation. Trying to get the disputants' emotions on the table can often move the hearing forward. If the disputants can express their anger or hurt, they can often focus better on the substantive issues. But in this case, Doreen takes it as a display of bias. Why?

When Sheila ends her story with a complaint about how she was treated by Doreen (excerpt seven), the mediator says, "It must really frustrate you." Because Doreen has not yet had a chance to tell her story, the mediator may have given Doreen the impression that she was accepting what Sheila was saying at face value (see also Rifkin, Millen, and Cobb, 1991). A few lines later, the mediator appears to align with Sheila's presentation of herself as weak and victimized (she had recently broken her leg). This alignment results in an implied criticism of Doreen, because Sheila is accusing Doreen of victimizing her.

Excerpt Seven

SHEILA: Yeah, I mean me and Doreen have been friends, you know, and I just, I just don't understand it, you know? It seems like . . .

MODERATOR: It must really frustrate [you].

SHEILA: [After I, well . . .] It was after I broke my leg, and you know . . . and [I d]on't know what happened! You . . . now we . . .

MODERATOR: So you're dealing with a broken leg [and it] . . .

SHEILA: [I was] dealing with a broken leg and then trying to deal with Doreen, you know? I was getting nowhere. [You] know? And I was just trying to be nice about it! You know?

MODERATOR: Do you miss her friendship?

The mediator again does emotion work with Sheila when she asks, "Do you miss her friendship?" With this utterance, the mediator seems to be trying to bring the emotional issues underlying the dispute to the surface. She may also be trying to get Sheila to say something nice about the other disputant, which can diffuse bad feelings and enable the disputants to move forward.

Excerpt eight shows an instance in Doreen's story in which the mediator missed a potential opportunity to do emotion work. Doreen is explaining some of the stresses she is under and why she does not want Sheila involved in her life any more. Instead of reflecting her feelings or expressing sympathy with the stresses she is under, the mediator chastises her for repeating herself and asks her to finish her story so that they can get back to Sheila.

Excerpt Eight

DOREEN: I feel like no matter what, out of all the things she's done . . . I can't be involved in that anymore. I have too many problems. I have five kids, I have three grand kids. And she was putting all this stress on me, all these problems. Telling me about her stealing all this money! I'm . . . I'm sorry, but I could not deal with it anymore. I don't want to be a part of it anymore! And when you know? I . . . all the tapes? And everything? I know Sheila tapes everything! That's not nothing new to me. She's done it forever! So, all those conversations, she may have a conversation with Andrew. But she's called my house numerous times. That conversation can be from last year.

MODERATOR: Eh, so [that] we don't get back into repeating ourselves about [the fact that] she tapes everything . . . and, you know, I['ve] heard that several times now . . . Is there anything new that you want to tell me right now? Be[fore we give Sheila a chance] to res[pond?]

In sum, the imbalanced use of emotion work with the disputants may have led Doreen to feel as though the mediator was ignoring her emotions, and, consequently, it may have contributed to her accusation of mediator bias.

Domenici and Littlejohn (2001) remind mediators that it is important to pay attention to emotions: "The emotional part of the conflict often needs an emotion-venting period before the rational, content-related issues can be explored" (p. 118). (See also Mackie, Miles, Marsh, and Allen, 2000.) However, they note that it is important to pay attention to the *intensity* of emotions as well. In this hearing, the mediator may have erred not only by focusing on Sheila's emotions extensively while slighting Doreen's but also by underestimating the intensity of Doreen's emotions. Some disputants do a better job of hiding or containing their emotions than others. But the fact that a person is not expressing emotions does not mean that he or she is not experiencing them. Perhaps mediators should consider explicitly asking disputants about their emotions at the beginning of the hearing, to get an idea of how to handle them during the hearing and to get those emotions on the table.

In sum, our conclusion from the analysis of these data is that the bias complaint emerged primarily because the mediator's attempts to empower an apparently weaker disputant backfired when the other disputant interpreted these actions as bias against her. The mediator used different story solicitations, different questions, and different interventions during the stories, as well as different completion queries and different amounts of emotion work, which led Doreen to feel that the mediator was siding with Sheila and her claims.

Discussion

Mediators must constantly think about how their responses to one disputant will be perceived by the other. The mediator's job is a delicate one and is fraught with difficulties. Some of these difficulties became apparent in the hearing analyzed in this article. In this section, we summarize these findings and we recommend questions for further research. We also make some suggestions for mediators to consider as they use empowerment and other techniques in their practice.

The Appearance of Asymmetry

A key element in this hearing was the use of various mediator techniques to offer support to an apparently weaker disputant in an attempt to empower her. Valid mediator techniques, such as summarizing disputants' stories, representing disputants' positions to one another, and doing emotion work, created a perception of bias in a disputant because they were applied in a way that appeared unequal.

Because mediators do not typically inform disputants that they are using techniques such as empowerment or emotion work, it is especially important that they consider how a disputant might perceive these actions as displaying bias. Disputants are not necessarily aware of the reasons behind many of these techniques, or even that they are being used. In this hearing, we found that the mediator used empowering techniques for Sheila because she assessed her as being the more needy disputant. But because Doreen did not know that that was why the mediator was giving her this help, she interpreted it as bias against her.

Perhaps mediators should first discuss the empowerment technique with the disputants to make sure that they know what is being done so that they will not misinterpret it as bias and so that they can correctly inform the mediator about what needs for assistance each of them has during the hearing. In the current case, empowerment might have been withheld until after the mediator had a chance to interact (at least briefly) with both disputants and assess the relative strengths and weaknesses of each. This case indicates that providing each disputant with the opportunity to give a brief description of her problem before either begins her "long story" might attenuate bias perceptions. Or mediators could have a brief informal exchange with the disputants before the hearing starts. Another option might be to directly ask each disputant what her or his strengths and weaknesses are and what type of help each would like during the hearing. While including disputants in the decision may be more ethical than using empowerment as an undercover technique, this type of public discussion of a disputant's weaknesses may not always be feasible or desirable.

If further research finds that asymmetry in treatment related to empowerment techniques is related to perceptions of bias, mediators might want to sensitize themselves as to how story interventions—for example, supportive continuers, informational questions, and topic redirects—can be used, while avoiding creating a perception of bias. As in the case discussed here, not all disputants need the same kind of interventions, so they should not simply be treated in exactly the same way. But care could be taken to avoid differences in substance or in tone—for example, displaying skepticism of one disputant's claims while treating the other's as true or neutral. This case suggests that the mediator's strategy of "replacing the disputant" by challenging one disputant's story on the other's behalf (Garcia, 1995) might be questionable. If disputants make their own critiques of each other's stories, mediators can avoid appearing to take sides. In addition, this case indicates that completion queries should provide the same degree of latitude for each disputant to add to her or his story, repeat points, or add new evidence or new complaints.

The Organization of the Mediation Hearing

Whereas the organization of mediation hearings differs depending on the program, mediator style, and type of mediation, a common mediation structure is one in which disputants tell their initial stories in turn, without fear of being interrupted by the other party (Garcia, 1991; see Greatbatch and Dingwall, 1997, on other ways of organizing mediation). The opposing disputant is thus excluded from the interaction during the story. This organization allows each disputant to tell her or his side of the story without interruption and works to minimize arguments (Garcia, 1991), but it can also create an awkward environment for the disputant who is not currently speaking. Because opposing disputants' versions of the same story will most likely differ, the mediator must elicit as much information as possible from each in order to fully understand both sides of the dispute. This can leave one person out of the process of interaction for an extended period of time. During this time, this person is typically not allowed to react to what is being discussed by the other disputant and the mediator; nor is he or she allowed to immediately object to or refute any information currently being discussed. This may lead to the appearance that the mediator is aligned with the disputant who is currently telling his or her story. Therefore, mediators need to be alert as to how their actions might be perceived in this context.

The problem with bias uncovered in this article suggests that some disputants may feel biased against when a mediator takes a long time to interact with the opposing disputant, before they have had a chance to tell any of their story. The mediator can minimize this risk by how he or she talks to the other disputant—for example, taking a provisional stance toward her or his utterance, or occasionally reminding both disputants that each will get a chance to tell her or his version of events. The mediator can remind the disputants that each disputant's story is not taken as fact by the mediator; it is just that disputant's version. Some mediators ask the "listening" disputant to make a written note of any issues in the other disputant's story that he or she may wish to respond to. This allows the listening disputant some assurance of getting an opportunity to convey her or his disagreements. And by the act of writing at specific points in the storyteller's story, the listening disputant is able to show *what* he or she disagrees with. This enables the listening disputant to communicate a disagreement without speaking or interrupting the storytelling disputant. Another approach—perhaps a little more intrusive of the story—would be to allow the opposing disputant to speak to register a disagreement. That disagreement would be noted, and the opposing disputant would address it later. But the fact that a disagreement had been clearly registered might affect both the storyteller's telling of her or his story and the listening disputant's feeling of involvement with the process.

Mediators might also consider using a collaborative storytelling process. The mediator could focus on the chronology of events and ask each disputant to tell what he or she did at each step in the process. For example, Disputant A might say, "I brought my car to Bob's repair shop to have the engine fixed." And then Disputant B responds, "We had our technician work on it, but the job turned out to be more complicated than we had thought." In short, both participants would be involved in constructing the narrative, and the mediator would facilitate and perhaps draw a timeline of events on the board, using symbols for diverging perspectives.

Mediators could also allow either disputant to call a time-out at any point in the mediation to discuss the process of the interaction if they are uncomfortable with the way things are being handled or confused about what should happen next. They could also allow disputants to call caucuses, as well as mediators. Disputants might then be able to raise with the mediator, in private, any questions of potential bias.

The "Dominance" of the First Story

This case indicates that asymmetry in story solicits may be problematic—especially asymmetry that appears to critique the second story using the logic and/or facts from the first story. For example, at the beginning of the hearing, the mediator could say, "Each of you will explain what happened from your point of view. Disputant A, we agreed that you would go first." And when Disputant A's story is over, the mediator could say, "Thank you for explaining what happened from your point of view. Now it is Disputant B's turn to explain what happened from his or her point of view."

Getting both disputants involved in the decision of who will present his or her case first might preempt any feelings of unfairness if the first story ends up seeming too long. In some mediation programs, there is a policy that the person who brought the complaint to mediation is the first one to "tell their story." If this is the case, the disputants should be informed that this is why one party is asked to go first. If there is no convention regarding who will go first, an arbitrary method such as a coin toss could be used to determine who starts.

Emotion Work

As shown in the preceding analysis, there was unequal treatment of the two disputants with regard to how their expressions of feeling were treated. The mediator picked up on Sheila's expressions of emotion and responded to them, whereas, for the most part, she ignored Doreen's expressions of emotions. This difference in treatment may have contributed to Doreen's bias complaint. It also seems that the mediator may have erred in her assessment of the needs of the two participants; she may have underestimated the intensity of Doreen's emotions, perhaps because of her apparent plan to empower Sheila. We have discussed the empowerment technique else-where, so we will not revisit it here, but we will briefly consider a couple of possible alternatives the mediator could have used in this hearing. If dis-putants do not make their emotional states clear at the beginning of the hearing, perhaps the mediator could ask them to rate their intensity of emotion on a scale of one to ten, as a way of getting a rough estimate of how volatile the situation is. Or the mediator could ask them how comfortable they are communicating with each other, as a way of gauging potential problems requiring emotion work.

Implications for Research and Practice

By examining an actual bias complaint as it unfolds, we can learn things about how an accusation of nonneutrality can arise that cannot be learned by other types of research, such as surveys or questionnaires. The examina-tion of the actual interaction as it occurs during the mediation hearing can offer a richer view into the ways in which perceptions of nonneutrality can arise.

Further research should be done to determine whether the findings of this analysis apply more generally. A collection of tapes of mediation hearings could be obtained, with the participants being given a survey fol-lowing the hearing that will gauge their perceptions about the fairness of the process and the potential for mediator bias. Then, a conversation ana-lytic study of the tapes could be done to see if asymmetry of treatment is related to perceptions of bias. The ideal way of conducting this research would be to use the "impact" method (Frankel and Beckman, 1982), whereby participants are shown a videotape of the hearing they have just participated in and are asked to stop the tape where they see problems hap-pening and then record their comments on the interaction. This would enable us to map each disputant's perceptions of unfairness or bias with specific mediator actions and other events in the hearings. Disputant responses to different mediation techniques could be compared.

This case raises several central questions for the practice of mediation. First, how does asymmetry in story solicitations, story interventions, and other techniques shape perceptions of disputants? The evidence presented here suggests that asymmetry that appears to critique the second story using the logic or facts from the first story should be avoided. Second, how might involving disputants in the decision to use empowerment techniques affect perceptions of unequal treatment? Third, how does the organization of the hearing relate to perceptions of bias? Might disputants experience more equality of treatment if they are allowed some type of intervention in the opposing disputant's story—for example, permission to register a complaint or call a caucus? Fourth, would reorganizing the mediation process minimize the dominance of the first disputant's story? This case suggests that getting both disputants involved in the decision of who will present her or his case first might have facilitated a successful mediation. Fifth, could giving greater attention to each disputant's emotions reduce perceptions of bias? The answers to these questions should help mediators maintain a perception of equality of treatment in the minds of the disputants.

References

Atkinson, J. M., and Heritage, J. (eds.). *Structure of Social Action: Studies in Conversation Analysis.* Cambridge, U.K.: Cambridge University Press, 1984.

Bahr, S. "Mediation Is the Answer: Why Couples Are So Positive About This Route to Divorce." *Family Advocate,* 1981, *3* (4), 32–35.

Barsky, A. E. "Mediation and Empowerment in Child Protection Cases." *Mediation Quarterly,* 1996, *14* (2), 111–134.

Benjamin, M., and Irving, H. "Research in Family Mediations: Review and Implications." *Mediation Quarterly,* 1995, *13* (1), 53–82.

Chandler, D. B. "Violence, Fear, and Communication: The Variable Impact of Domestic Violence of Mediation." *Mediation Quarterly,* 1990, *7* (4), 331–346.

Cobb, S., and Rifkin, J. "Neutrality as a Discursive Practice: The Construction and Transformation of Narratives in Community Mediation." *Law, Politics, and Society,* 1991, *11,* 69–81.

Depner, C. E., Cannata, K. B., and Simon, M. B. "Building a Uniform Statistical Reporting System: A Snapshot of California Family Court Services." *Family and Conciliation Courts Review,* 1992, *30* (2), 185–206.

Domenici, K., and Littlejohn, S. W. *Mediation: Empowerment in Conflict Management.* Prospect Heights, Ill.: Waveland Press, 2001.

Donohue, W. A. "Communicative Competence in Mediators." In K. Kressel, D. G. Pruitt, and Associates (eds.), *Mediation Research: The Process and Effectiveness of Third-Party Intervention.* San Francisco: Jossey-Bass, 1989.

Frankel, R. M., and Beckman, H. B. "Impact: An Interaction-Based Method for Preserving and Analyzing Clinical Transactions." In L. Pettigrew (ed.), *Explorations in Provider and Patient Interactions.* Nashville, Tennessee: Humana, 1982.

Garcia, A. C. "Dispute Resolution Without Disputing: How the Interactional Organization of Mediation Hearings Minimizes Argument." *American Sociological Review,* 1991, *56,* 818–835.

Garcia, A. C. "The Problematics of Representation in Community Mediation Hearings: Implications for Mediation Practice." *Journal of Sociology and Social Welfare,* 1995, *22* (4), 23–46.

Gaughan, R. A. "The Family Mediation Service." In H. Davidson, and Associates (eds.), *Alternative Means of Family Dispute Resolution.* Washington, D.C.: American Bar Association, 1982.

Gaybrick, A., and Bryner, D. "Mediation in a Public Setting: Arlington, Virginia." *Family Law Reporter,* Apr. 14, 1981.

Greatbatch, D., and Dingwall, R. "Argumentative Talk in Divorce Mediation Sessions." *American Sociological Review,* 1997, *62,* 151–70.

Harrington, C. B. *Shadow Justice: The Ideology and Institutionalization of Alternatives to Court.* Westport, Conn.: Greenwood Press, 1985.

Irving, H. H., and Benjamin, M. "An Evaluation of Process of Outcome in a Private Family Mediation Service." *Mediation Quarterly,* 1992, *10* (1), 35–55.

Kelly, J. B. "Mediated and Adversarial Divorce: Respondents' Perceptions of Their Processes and Outcomes." In J. B. Kelly (ed.), *Empirical Research in Divorce and Family Mediation.* Mediation Quarterly, no. 24. San Francisco: Jossey-Bass, 1989.

Kelly, J. B., and Duryee, M. A. "Women's and Men's Views of Mediation in Voluntary and Mandatory Settings." *Family and Conciliation Courts Review,* 1992, *30* (1), 34–49.

Mackie, K., Miles, D., Marsh, W., and Allen, T. *The ADR Practice Guide to Commercial Dispute Resolution.* London: Butterworths, 2000.

Matz, D. E. "Mediator Pressure and Party Autonomy—Are They Consistent with Each Other?" *Negotiation Journal,* 1994, *10* (4), 359–365.

Meierding, N. R. "Does Mediation Work? A Survey of Long-Term Satisfaction of Divorce Mediating Couples." *Mediation Quarterly,* 1993, *11* (2), 157–170.

Mellinger, W. M. "The Production of Organizational Records: The Complaint-Taker's Construction of the 'Dispatch Package.'" Unpublished manuscript, 1989.

Neumann, D. "How Mediation Can Effectively Address the Male-Female Power Imbalance in Divorce." *Mediation Quarterly,* 1992, *9* (3), 227–239.

Parker, A. O., Jr. "A Comparison of Divorce Mediation Versus Lawyer Adversary Processes and the Relationship to Marital Separation." Unpublished doctoral dissertation, University of North Carolina, 1980.

Pearson, J., and Thoennes, N. "A Preliminary Portrait of Client Reactions to Three Court Mediation Programs." *Conciliation Courts Review,* 1985, *23* (1), 1–14.

Regehr, C. "The Use of Empowerment in Child Custody Mediation: A Feminist Critique." *Mediation Quarterly,* 1994, *11* (4), 361–371.

Rifkin, J., Millen, J., and Cobb, S. "Toward a New Discourse for Mediation: A Critique of Neutrality." *Mediation Quarterly,* 1991, *9* (2), 151–164.

Roehl, J. A., and Cook, R. F. "Mediation in Interpersonal Disputes: Effectiveness and Limitations." In K. Kressell, D. G. Pruitt, and Associates (eds.), *Mediation Research: The Process and Effectiveness of Third-Party Intervention.* San Francisco: Jossey-Bass, 1989.

Sacks, H., Schegloff, E., and Jefferson, G. "A Simplest Systematics for the Organization of Turn-Taking for Conversation." *Language,* 1974, *50* (4), 696–735.

Saposnek, D. T., Hamburg, J., Delano, C. D., and Michaelson, H. "How Has Mandatory Mediation Fared? Research Findings of the First Year's Follow-Up." *Family and Conciliation Courts Review,* 1984, *22* (2), 7–19.

Stulberg, J. B. "The Theory and Practice of Mediation: A Reply to Professor Susskind." *Vermont Law Review,* 1981, *6* (1), 49–116.

Susskind, L. "Environmental Mediation and the Accountability Problem." *Vermont Law Review,* 1981, *6* (1), 1–48.

Thoennes, N. A., and Pearson, J. "Predicting Outcomes in Divorce Mediation: The Influence of People and Process." *Journal of Social Issues,* 1985, *41* (2), 115–126.

Tjosvold, D., and Van de Vliert, E. "Applying Cooperation and Competitive Conflict Theory to Mediation." *Mediation Quarterly,* 1994, *11* (4), 303–311.

Ury, W. *Getting Past No: Negotiating Your Way from Confrontation to Cooperation.* New York: Bantam, 1993.

Waldron, J. A., and others. "A Therapeutic Mediation Model for Child Custody Dispute Resolution." In J. A. Lemmon (ed.), *Reaching Effective Agreements.* San Francisco: Jossey-Bass, 1984.

Wall, J. A., Jr. "Mediation: An Analysis, Review, and Proposed Research." *Journal of Conflict Resolution,* 1981, *16,* 51–65.

Whalen, M., and Zimmerman, D. H. "Describing Trouble: Practical Epistemology in Citizen Calls to the Police." *Language and Society,* 1990, *19,* 465–492.

Angela Cora Garcia is an associate professor in the Department of Sociology at the University of Cincinnati. Her research includes qualitative studies of the interactional organization of mediation hearings, moral reasoning in mediation, how proposals and offers are presented and negotiated in mediation, and how accusations of mediator bias can arise.

Kristie Vise is a research analyst in the sociology department at Northern Kentucky University. She specializes in program evaluation for the nonprofit sector.

Stephen Paul Whitaker is a doctoral student at the Institute for Women's Studies at Emory University in Atlanta. His interests include sociological research on "everyday" interaction.

Discourses in the Use and Emergence of Organizational Conflict

IWONA L. KUSZTAL

Four discourses in use were identified in a grounded theory study of organizational conflict. This article discusses how these different discourses in use were involved in the emergence of organizational conflicts. Discourses in use determine what conflicts arise in the organization and how they are understood and managed. In this article, the practical implication of this approach for assessing and managing conflict processes in organizations is considered.

Little is known about how organizational conflicts emerge. When one starts with situations that have already escalated, it is difficult to retrace the process. For the participants, the present always colors the past, and what happened earlier is difficult to re-create. Therefore, it is important to study organizational conflicts when they first emerge. Many start out small and are soon forgotten. Others linger on and, over time, may become more serious problems. We need to know more about the emergent nature of organizational conflict and how conflict gets transformed in the process of organizational interaction. This knowledge can be crucial for successful conflict management and, in some cases, prevention.

A grounded theory study was conducted to explore how the process occurs naturally in the organizational setting. The study pursued the following research questions: (1) How do organizational members come to understand their problematic experience through discourse, and how are problematic situations noticed, labeled, and experienced? (2) How does members' understanding affect the way they deal with the problem, and, in reciprocal fashion, what consequences do their actions have for organizational practice and individual and collective understandings within the organization? (3) How are members' understanding of problematic situations transformed in the process of organizational interaction? and (4) What role do individual and collective understandings play in conflict emergence and transformation?

Theoretical Background

To give the inquiry general focus and direction, the study integrated insights from Felstiner, Abel, and Sarat's model of dispute transformation (1980–81), Weick's theory of organizational sensemaking (1995), Giddens's structuration theory (1979, 1993, 1994), and interpretive sociolegal research that focused on discursive processes in dispute transformation (Greenhouse, Yngvesson, and Engel, 1994; Mather and Yngvesson, 1980–81; Merry, 1990; Yngvesson, 1976, 1978, 1988, 1993). Based on the reviewed literature, a discourse-focused approach was developed. This section briefly outlines this approach.

Felstiner, Abel, and Sarat (1980–81) view conflict as emergent. Conflict arises when individuals notice certain situations as being injurious or problematic. Their understanding evolves in the process of social interaction, and it influences how they deal with the problem. The researchers urge for the study of conflict transformations or "the way in which experiences become grievances, grievances become disputes, and disputes take various shapes, follow particular dispute processing paths, and lead to new forms of understanding" (p. 632). The process of conflict transformation, according to the researchers, is *subjective,* because transformation may just involve changes in interpretation or feelings and may not be directly apparent in a social actor's behavior. The process is *unstable,* in that the transformations may occur repeatedly and the social actor's view of what happened may keep changing over time. The process is *reactive,* because individuals redefine their perceptions and modify their behavior in response to the communication, behavior, and expectations of many different people, including opponents, intimates, agents, lawyers, and superiors. Finally, the process has a tendency to *avoid closure* because new claims often emerge, and conflicts, apparently resolved, may resurface.

The study proposed that the conflict dynamic be conceptualized as a discursive process of organizational sensemaking. Sensemaking can be broadly defined as a retrospective process of creating sense in the evolving interaction (Weick, 1995). Giddens's idea of duality of structure (1979, 1993, 1994) was used to better explain the reciprocal connection between members' understanding and actions. Members' discourse was treated as an important link between the two. Focus on discourse helped connect key concepts and dimensions into a well-integrated whole. The following paragraphs present the underlying assumptions of this view and their implications for the study of organizational conflict.

Across the theories, discourse is considered the principle means by which individuals make sense of and construct their social reality. To make sense of organizational events, organizational members retrospectively apply categories of discourse to the flow of organizational action that is otherwise equivocal, puzzling, and uncertain. So discourse in use is both the means and the expression of members' understanding. Members construct their understanding through discourse, and in the process of their interactions, they re-create their organizational reality. The focus on discourse as the means and outcome of members' sensemaking enables one to systematically study the conflict dynamic in terms of organizational members' evolving understanding and action.

The study of members' sensemaking as a discursive phenomenon helps bridge the individual and collective dimensions of the process. Again, Giddens's idea of structuration was used to explain that connection. Discourse, as a structural property of the system, is tied to members' organizational practices. In the process of their everyday interactions, members construct in discourse an accountable universe of meaning that makes their organizational practices make sense. Members' discourse is considered the means through which collective understanding is reconstituted in situated actions or accounts of individuals. The systematic analysis of members' discourse can provide valuable insights into the patterns of collective understanding in the organization and how they are reconstituted in individuals' processes of sensemaking.

This view of discourse is consistent with a number of interpretive sociolegal studies that focus on the processes of dispute transformation in local communities (Greenhouse, Yngvesson, and Engel, 1994; Mather and Yngvesson, 1980–81; Merry, 1990; Yngvesson, 1976, 1978, 1988, 1993). The studies examine how, in the process of conflict interaction, different discourses come to bear on social actors' understanding and actions and transform the conflict. Conflict transformation is conceptualized here as a discourse-driven process. This approach has many implications for the study of organizational conflict.

The analysis of members' discourse across time and space enables one to trace spatial and temporal transformations in organizational understanding. Organizational situations that are seen as problematic may represent potential transformation points for the individuals and the organization. They may represent discontinuities between individual and collective understanding, understanding and action, and organizational past and present. Discourse is the means of managing these discontinuities. The way problematic situations are managed across time will have important consequences for what the organization and its members become.

Methodology

The site of this research was an administrative department of a large urban university in the Northeast. The university is a publicly funded research institution that serves over twenty-eight thousand students. The department, here called the Office, was responsible for development, scheduling, and operation of campus programs, activities, and social events. The Office was made up of eight full-time staff members, all of whom participated in the study. In addition, the department employed graduate assistants as part-time staff members, and three of them participated in the study.

The data collection at the site was conducted over a ten-month period and employed open-ended qualitative interviewing and observation. The interview sessions were scheduled roughly every two to three weeks, depending on the availability of the participants. Altogether, 136 interviews were conducted. Roughly one to two hours per week were spent observing members' informal interactions and staff meetings; the latter were also recorded.

The interviews focused on what the participants indicated were problematic situations encountered on the job. The participants were asked to bring up any situations that were in some way agitating or frustrating to them personally or that involved other members of the staff. They were encouraged to talk freely and at length about what had happened and how they had experienced it. Before they moved on to talk about another situation, questions were asked to clarify what was said and to seek additional information. Toward the end of the interview, follow-up questions were asked about the situations that participants had brought up during previous sessions.

The interviews were transcribed word for word, with hesitation, false starts, and longer pauses also being marked. The transcripts were arranged chronologically, and discourse sequences were marked to indicate the problematic incidents and subsequent accounts thereof. A chronological list of problematic incidents was generated that indicated the spatial and temporal spans of conflicts—that is, who brought them up, when, and over what period of time. It helped identify the conflicts that were more salient. Spatial and temporal spans were treated as important properties of conflicts as a general category. The list was also a useful tool for navigating the expanding data set.

The process of data analysis was ongoing throughout the research process. It followed the general guidelines of grounded theory (Strauss and Corbin, 1990; Glaser, 1978; Glaser and Strauss, 1967; Strauss, 1987; Strauss and Corbin, 1990, 1994). During the early stages of data analysis, close, line-by-line reading was used to uncover as many potentially relevant categories as possible. Subsequently, the readings became more selective and focused more closely on particular conflicts. The categories became more abstract and better developed as more cases were analyzed and contrasted. Four discourses in use were eventually identified as the highest-order categories. The analysis then concentrated on elaborating and refining the relationships between the categories and the subcategories.

Research Findings

Situations in which organizational members noticed that certain organizational occurrences were problematic were considered as instances of conflict emergence. The study focused mainly on the role of discourse in this conflict dynamic. Though conflicts can emerge from nondiscursive factors, they remain outside the purview of the study and are not discussed here. The study located the emergence of organizational conflict almost exclusively in the use of discourse. This was consistent with the study's interest in the processes of organizational sensemaking, for it is in one's sensemaking of the conflict through discourse that the conflict becomes a social entity and is enacted as such.

Discourse analysis revealed four different discourses in use. At the site studied, members used the managerial discourse of bureaucracy, professional discourse, human connection discourse, and political discourse to make sense of their organizational reality. The four discourses in use reconstituted members' collective understanding in everyday office interactions. They enabled members to coordinate their actions in meaningful ways and to function relatively smoothly as an organization. But the four discourses in use also lay at the basis of organizational conflicts. Giddens's model of duality of structure helped capture the systematic differences between the four discourses in use, in terms of their underlying structures of signification, legitimation, and domination. On the level of members' interaction, the four discourses in use relied on (1) different sets of meanings, with attention focused on different issues, casting them in different terms, (2) members' roles being framed differently, as they determined who the relevant parties were, structuring their capacity for involvement, (3) the reproduction of different types of relationships between members, and (4) the suggestion of different types of "solutions," or courses of "appropriate" action.

Managerial Discourse of Bureaucracy

When managerial discourse of bureaucracy was used, the staff members considered their own and others' actions in terms of formal organizational structure—that is, policies and procedures, job responsibilities, task assignments, and reporting lines. A violation of these formal structures by student organizations, other departments, or the staff members themselves was what made situations problematic in terms of managerial discourse. When such violation was noticed, the staff members referred to organizational policies, procedures, and job responsibilities to better determine the nature of the problem—that is, what the problem was about, whose responsibility it was, and how it was to be managed. For example, Ron, who was the adviser to student organizations and who reported to Sally, made the following observation about problems in his area: "Based upon the rules and regulations of the university and of this department, red flags go up at different times. If students in their organization are getting ready to do some things that are counter to the university rules, and it looks like it's gonna affect some things, then I bring it up and get Sally's advice on how I should proceed."

Managerial discourse was associated with the use of formal roles in organizational interaction. When members used managerial discourse, they acted as occupants of a certain formal position—for example, as the director, office manager, or programmer. Their interaction reconstituted formal hierarchical relationships. It was understood that superiors had formal control over and responsibility for the units they supervised. Their subordinates were expected to keep them informed, seek their direction, and follow their decisions. Managerial discourse was not a participatory discourse. Parties' involvement was restricted by organizational procedures and it decreased down the organizational hierarchy.

Framing problems in managerial discourse suggested the use of proper organizational channels and procedures. When members failed in their responsibilities, it was up to their immediate supervisor to deal with the problem and get them in line. The supervisor would evaluate their performance, restructure responsibilities, give oral or written warnings, and use other forms of formal control or discipline.

Discourse of Professionalism

When discourse of professionalism was used, organizational situations were understood in terms of more diverse and less explicit standards of professionalism. The emphasis shifted from whether or not organizational members did their job to how they did it. Based on their professional expertise, job experience, and work ethics, members often believed that certain situations should be managed differently. They felt that others used poor professional judgment, were being inefficient or ineffective in their jobs, and needed to be more creative or innovative, take more initiative, and be more supportive of the department and more involved in its operations. In the following fragment, a participant used professional discourse to express her frustration with Carol, the office manager: "We (the office) run okay now, but I think if I were an office manager, I would be constantly thinking of ways to improve the office, ways to improve the organization of cabinets and stuff like that, and ways to make most of the use of our students. If that were my job, then I think I would take more pride in coming up with some systems or improvements. I don't think Carol feels the need to do that, or even wants to."

In terms of their role, members acted as professionals, and, as team players, they often went "beyond the call." They emphasized the need for continuous professional development and growth. Professional expertise and initiative, passionate involvement in what one was doing, and adherence to high standards of performance were seen as very important aspects of who they were as professionals. When professional discourse was used, it reconstituted a collegial relationship. Members felt that they could approach others as colleagues and equals to raise important issues. Professional discourse fostered involvement and participation. For example, one participant observed, "Professionals need to sit down and say, 'This is what we need you to do. Do you realize that you may not be doing this or that you may be doing too much of this and not enough of this? And do you realize that . . . ?' . . . because things can look different . . . from somebody else's shoes, and ultimately, I think *that* is where any group needs to spend its time. I mean, if they . . . if people are gonna grow and not be hurt about things, you know. . . ."

Professional discourse in use suggested collegial solutions. Based on their commitment to the department, others felt the need to get involved and make the employee aware of the problems. They tried to understand the professional basis of his or her difficulties, what he or she was doing wrong, and what might help. They suggested certain systems and solutions, offered assistance, and tried to help the employee improve.

Discourse of Human Connection

When human connection discourse was used, members understood problematic situations in terms of commonsense understandings that were drawn from the general culture of everyday life and pertained to the "proper" way of being in the world. The issues raised had to do with other people being insensitive, inconsiderate of their feelings and special needs, unable or unwilling to understand them, and unwilling to consider their special circumstances or offer personal support. They failed to show basic human respect, empathy, maturity, and common sense.

When human connection discourse was used, members acted in their private capacity as human beings. Human connection discourse emphasized the commonness of human connection as the basis for relating to others. It reinforced the human capacity to understand and empathize with other people's problems, circumstances, and life situations. In the following fragment, a member used human connection discourse when he talked about the student staff member who reported the office manager.

> They are not staying busy, . . . you know they sit a lot. . . . I don't think it's healthy. I really want to see these students being very productive, always moving, doing things. As a parent, I taught my children the same principles with house chores. I believe that if children learn house chores, they are learning life skills, and I look at this office in the same way. If they learn how to consistently do things, they're learning life skills, so when they walk out of there they have gained some skills, you know. I am interested in seeing youngsters learn skills and have good manners and appreciate people, not just because of the way they look or the color of their skin but because of the character of their heart. And the person who teaches that has to have a good heart. A person with a bad heart can't teach another person how to have a good heart. It's almost like you have to walk the walk and talk the talk.

Human connection discourse in use fostered members' involvement and participation, particularly when members acted as friends. They would often turn to others to seek support and vent their frustrations. Problems framed in human connection discourse suggested an informal, personal type of solutions–for example, providing personal help and support, being truthful and honest, and hearing others out. But curtailing the relationship instead of repairing it was sometimes also a viable option, particularly when one was just too angry or too hurt, and when the connection was lost because the other appeared to be so unlike oneself—was inconsiderate, dishonest, rude, lazy, or stupid. That was usually communicated nonverbally by limiting interaction, withdrawing, withholding acknowledgement during informal encounters, and so forth.

Political Discourse

When political discourse was used, problematic situations were seen in terms of members' threatened interests and underlying differences of power: "This is a dog-eat-dog kind of world," one staff member explained. "You need to be smart in order to survive." "Being smart" meant making the "right" moves and saying the "right" things—things that were not necessarily true or honest but that would get you what you needed or wanted. In the following fragment, a staff member used political discourse to talk about an upper administration person:

> Dr. Taylor makes assumptions of people with very, very, very limited information, which is very scary, but she does. So, if she walked into this office, I don't care how bad your day is, you have to be on, you have to be. I don't care, if . . . you know, you just have to act like . . . you know, like "I love my life, I love my job, and give me, give me, give me, I'll do anything." . . . That's the attitude she wants, and if she doesn't get it, then she assumes that you're that way all the time, and "I don't need you."

When members used political discourse, they emphasized the need to be politically smart and they took on the role of strategists or political players. In the majority of cases, members used political discourse when dealing with interoffice conflicts that involved other departments and higher administration. In those situations, political discourse in use reconstituted a "we against them" orientation that fostered intragroup connection. Things changed, however, when members sensed that others were playing their own games, and political discourse was being used more frequently in intraoffice conflicts. When that happened, a sense of distrust and suspicion permeated the office and transformed members' relationships.

Framing problems in political discourse made power imbalance between the parties particularly salient and called for a well-calculated strategy. Members felt that they had to be very careful about what they said, how they said it, and to whom: "Some things you don't bring up, you don't talk about them, you cover your tracks. . . . A lot of times I choose not to tell people things that they don't need to know," one member said. Or, "Sometimes, you let stuff out, because you want it leaked," another member observed. To stay on top of the game, members relied on a range of formal and informal resources that were available to them. In the process, they often appropriated the other discourses appealing to formal policies, professionalism, and personal, human ties. Their rationale, however, was based on political discourse, and their objective was to gain advantage or just survive in this game of organizational politics.

Members' accounts showed that it was members' inability to make sense of a situation as others did that often led to conflict. The majority of conflicts emerged when members used different discourses. They understood organizational situations differently; that is, (1) they focused on different issues and cast them in different terms, (2) they adopted different roles, (3) they acted on the basis of a different type of relationship, and (4) their actions, or solutions, made sense to them but were often problematic from the perspective of the others.

The two discourses that most frequently functioned in opposition to each other were managerial discourse and professional discourse. When members used professional discourse, they often resisted formal managerial structures and actions; they found them stifling and limiting. As professionals, they expected a more collegial relationship. For example, a member recalled a problematic interaction with her boss: "His position is 'I'm the director, and whatever I say goes.' What I'm noticing more and more is that he's questioning every single thing we do. . . . When he is on a rampage . . . And if there's a situation that comes up, he's gonna question, you know, your professionalism, your competency, all of that, you know?"

When members used professional discourse, they often sidestepped or challenged formal organizational procedures and policies. This presented problems for them and others, in terms of managerial discourse. In the following fragment, an employee talks about a decision he had made, which his boss later saw as problematic:

> I didn't want to make the student organization get all these four groups
> to get a review, write up a new constitution, and go through all this

extra . . . you know, just to set up a Web page. . . . That's why I made my judgment call. . . . I was real upset that he felt he had to lecture me about why he thought that was a bad decision, and I was just . . . I was just trying to get the student organization taken care of, get them in and get them out . . . and, you know, serve them, as opposed to being a disservice to them.

Managerial discourse and human connection discourse also functioned in opposition in some situations. Members who used managerial discourse attended less to personal, human dimensions of the situation—others' feelings, needs, and special personal circumstances. For example, a supervisor confronted her subordinate when he missed a deadline: "I really don't care if he has to stay here till nine or ten . . . till it's done, and I told him that. I really don't care . . . whatever it takes, and I don't want to hear his excuses." Managerial actions were often seen as insensitive and inconsiderate by staff members, who expected more understanding and empathy. For example, one member remembered a meeting with her boss: "She was very cold, very cold, and kind of, well, formal, like: 'Give me this, give me that. Let's just get through this.'"

Human connection discourse and professional discourse in use lead to conflict less often. When members used human connection discourse, they were generally more understanding of their own and other people's follies. Professional discourse in use, on the other hand, was more strict in its standards of professional behavior. For example, a member noted, "I know it's a casual Friday, but come on, we're not at the beach."

Managerial discourse and political discourse in use also lead to conflict on some occasions. When members used managerial discourse, they found political discourse in use quite problematic, particularly, when coming from their subordinates. They felt that the other told them what they wanted to hear and tried to cover things up; they could not trust the information they were getting. One of the directors reported the following conflict with an employee: "She just plays with words, you know? Before she went on vacation I asked her about the Graduate Assistants' applications, and she said she had asked Carol to set up those appointments. I asked Carol on Thursday, and she didn't know what I was talking about. So, now, she's covering her tracks and saying she's gonna make her calls today, you know? It's frustrating to me as a supervisor, because I don't believe what she says she's gonna do is actually gonna happen, because it doesn't, or it's always different than what she said prior."

Members, too, suspected that on occasion their superiors were being political with them. They did not trust their managerial discourse and responded with political actions of their own. An employee reported how he was "watching his back" after receiving a series of formal warnings: "Maybe in the last six months, I've been noticing little things. You know, maybe it's nothing, maybe it's just . . . this is his managing style. It's . . . I find in talking to people all around campus that there is a concern all over the place of how supervisors are handling employees, I've heard many stories, I've heard some frightening stories about how people are being set up—like having four, five of that kind of comment that might be equal to one written discipline. It's called a paper trail. It's a process of how people eliminate people. I don't think that's happening to me, but just in case, I watch my back, you know?"

Professional discourse and political discourse functioned in opposition in some office conflicts. Staff members who used professional discourse generally resented what they saw as political discourse being used unprofessionally and unethically. They found it highly objectionable that others were being political with them or with other people whom they owed professional consideration. In some cases, this caused them to lose respect for that person. Political discourse in use went against their sense of collegiality. A member reported how a coworker "tabled" the issue that he raised at a staff meeting. He and some other staff members were concerned that student workers out in the front office played on the Internet while servicing clients. They did not think it was a professional thing to do. He proposed that they install a password to control the access. He described the coworker's tabling of the issue at the staff meeting: "She's very good; she'll gather the floor in the meeting, sort of like own the conversation to the point that people don't want to go forward with it any more, and she will sort of find a way to sort of table it, make it seem a little more complicated than it really is, like my issue about the Internet was very simple: 'Do you want to put a password on there? We can put a password on there.' And then very quickly it became a different discussion; it was like an effort to confuse the issue."

The staff member who used political discourse may have felt on occasions that others were possibly using professional discourse as leverage against her in a political game they were playing. The staff member could either join them or fight them. There is no first-party account of this process, however. There is a third-party account provided by a staff member who commented on a fragile relationship between her immediate supervisor (Sally) and the head of the department (Robert): "Of course, she's going to agree with him. What's she gonna do, argue? Even if she did disagree with that, it wouldn't be in her best interest to say, 'Why, I don't agree with that,' you know? Right now, it's in her best interest to just say, 'Oh, yeah, that's a good idea, I'm all for it.'"

Human connection discourse and political discourse were particularly incompatible when used by the parties. When staff members used human connection discourse, they expected honesty, understanding, compassion, and caring. In political discourse, however, their actions were considered not very good strategy. In the following fragment, one of the directors recalled an interaction with a member of his staff:

> This is so funny. . . . He was late one day. He said, "Oh, I'm sorry I'm late. I overslept." And he proceeded to talk, and he said, "You know, I woke up really, really late, so then I went over to work out, and there was, like, no way I was gonna be at work on time." I'm like, "Wait. You woke up late, and you made a decision . . . you chose: 'Do I want to be late for work, or do I want to work out? Like which one should I give up?' I think you should've given up the workout, but if you chose not to, then don't tell your boss you did that, just say 'I overslept.'"

Actions considered political, from the perspective of human connection discourse, came across as morally objectionable, dishonest, manipulative, unfair, and malicious. In the following fragment, an employee wondered about her supervisor's true motives: "I'm not sure that all of his motives, you know, are for a greater good. I don't believe that, I don't believe that. I believe it's a lot of people in this university who were afraid for their jobs. It's instinct, instinct about when someone is being honest with you, you know?—a vibe that you get from anybody. Makes me distrustful and makes me believe that you're capable of the worst, and not only are you capable, but you're quite willing, you know, to see that through."

On some occasions, conflict emerged when parties used the same discourse. This was relatively rare, however. For example, parties who used human connection discourse were, on occasions, insulted or hurt by others' insensitive comments, jokes, and criticism. When parties used professional discourse, conflicts sometimes revolved around differences in their professional expertise and work experience, with one party criticizing the other's decisions or work practices. There were relatively few cases reported of conflicts that emerged when both parties used managerial discourse. The issues usually had to do with lateral and hierarchical transfer of responsibility when some less formalized aspects of organizational practice failed. When both parties used political discourse, conflict was assumed and opposition was expected. It was not necessarily considered problematic, but rather "the way things are."

Practical Implications

The model developed in the study directs attention to multiple discourses in use that function in organizations. Depending on their practice, organizations may appropriate a range of different discourses from the broader culture. The study offers a comprehensive analysis of the four discourses found at the site—namely, managerial discourse, professional discourse, human connection discourse, and political discourse. But organizations can appropriate other discourses as well—for example, therapeutic, religious, scientific, legal, and the like. The model can be adapted to include other discourses not discussed in this study.

Discourses in use can be effectively identified through the use of qualitative methodology. The study relied mainly on individual interviews, but focus groups can also be used with some caution.

Discourses in use lie at the basis of organizational conflicts. Having identified the discourses in use, we have a better idea of the different types of conflicts that are likely to emerge in the organization. The approach can be adopted to study intragroup conflicts within organizational offices, departments, or teams that use the same set of discourses, or they can be expanded to trace intergroup conflicts between organizational units that use different discourses. Furthermore, the model can be used to assess the potential match between different organizations in organizational mergers and acquisitions. Organizations that appropriate different discourses face different types of conflicts and deal with them differently. Also, with more research, the model can be tailored to target specific types of organizations—for example, educational institutions, corporations, nonprofit agencies, and the like.

With the proliferation of new organizational programs and systems—for example, management by objectives and total quality management systems, organizations are likely to further expand their vocabularies. These new discourses, however, are likely to bring with them new types of conflicts. The model can be used to assess the fit between the organization and new programs that it plans to adopt. This can help us identify potential problems and better prepare to address them when they arise.

Contemporary organizational research and practice stress the need for requisite variety or internal diversity that matches the complexity of organizational environments (Orton and Weick, 1990; Sutcliffe, 2001; Weick 2001). Multiple discourses in use, which allow for different ways of seeing and acting, can facilitate organizational learning and adaptation. In that sense, organizational conflicts serve an important function: they are opportunities for positive change and organizational development.

Discourses in use determine what conflicts emerge across the organization and how they are handled. Different discourses in use have different implications for members' involvement and participation. For example, members reported significantly more problems when they used professional discourse. They were also more likely to raise those issues. They had high expectations of self and others and were more attentive to what was going on around them. When members used managerial discourse, they appeared to notice fewer problems. They focused mainly on doing their jobs and were much less concerned with what others were doing or not doing. Relatively few of those problems were addressed—those that were managed by appropriate supervisors. Members reported relatively few conflicts that started as personal problems, yet they remained quite sensitive to instances of rude or inconsiderate behavior, and many conflicts became personal when members dealt ineffectively with the original issues (either managerial, professional, or political). Other members got involved as parties turned to others to commiserate or seek support. When political discourse was used, members attended particularly to those relationships that they saw as political. At the time, they would report quite a few situations that they felt were politically threatening to them or to the department. Many problematic situations reported earlier would take on new significance and be managed through political actions. This article does not deal with conflict transformations or with discursive shifts in how conflict is defined and enacted across time and space. The model, however, can be effectively used to trace these processes as well. It can help identify problems such as patterns of conflict avoidance or conflict escalation, and it can be used to design appropriate interventions or conflict management systems to help organizations deal more effectively with their conflicts.

Limitations of the Study

The retrospective nature of participants' reports posed some limitations, however. Although members' accounts were quite detailed at times and often included recalled dialogue, it was still difficult to reproduce the actual interaction, particularly when days, or sometimes weeks, had passed since it had happened. As a result, the study gained only limited insights into how discursive shifts were interactionally managed.

Another problem that had to do with participants' recall was that they were more likely to remember and report those conflict situations that were somehow significant to them. They reported minor problems only when they happened earlier that day or the day before.

Though it was important to be able to consider accounts provided by different parties, in some cases, only one side of the story was offered. Mostly for ethical reasons, the researcher chose not to inquire unless the participants themselves mentioned the conflict.

The research involved just one organizational site, which is a limitation in terms of the generalizability of its findings. Though the new model appears to have a lot of potential in terms of application across different organizational settings, it has not been tested in other contexts. The data were collected at an administrative unit of an academic institution. The four discourses identified at the site may not necessarily be found in other organizations. Depending on their practice, organizations may appropriate a range of different discourses from the general culture—such as discourses that are therapeutic, religious, scientific, or legal. The types of conflicts that emerge and the patterns of their transformations will also be different. They will also have different consequences for the organizations and their members in terms of issues, roles, relationships, and individual and collective identities.

References

Felstiner, W.L.F., Abel, R. L., and Sarat, A. "The Emergence and Transformation of Disputes: Naming, Blaming, Claming . . ." *Law & Society Review,* 1980–81, *15,* 631–654.

Giddens, A. *Central Problems in Social Theory. Action, Structure and Contradiction in Social Analysis.* Berkeley and Los Angeles: University of California Press, 1979.

Giddens, A. *New Rules of Sociological Method.* Cambridge, U.K.: Polity Press, 1993.

Giddens, A. *The Constitution of Society. Outline of the Theory of Structuration.* Berkeley and Los Angeles: University of California Press, 1994.

Glaser, B. *Theoretical Sensitivity.* Mill Valley, Calif.: Sociological Press, 1978.

Glaser, B., and Strauss, A. L. *The Discovery of Grounded Theory: Strategies for Qualitative Research.* Hawthorne, N.Y.: Aldine de Gruyter, 1967.

Greenhouse, C. J., Yngvesson, B., and Engel, D. M. *Law and Community in Three American Towns.* Ithaca, N.Y.: Cornell University Press, 1994.

Mather, L., and Yngvesson, B. "Language, Audience, and the Transformation of Disputes." *Law and Society,* 1980–81, *15,* 775–820.

Merry, S. E. *Getting Justice and Getting Even: Legal Consciousness Among Working-Class Americans.* Chicago: University of Chicago Press, 1990.

Orton, D., and Weick, K. E. "Loosely Coupled Systems: A Reconceptualization." *Academy of Management Review,* 1990, *15,* 203–223.

Strauss, A. L. *Qualitative Analysis for Social Scientists.* New York: Cambridge University Press, 1987.

Strauss, A. L., and Corbin, J. *Basis of Qualitative Research: Grounded Theory Procedures and Techniques.* Thousand Oaks, Calif.: Sage, 1990.

Strauss, A. L., and Corbin, J. "Grounded Theory Methodology: An Overview." In N. K. Denizen, and Y. S. Lincoln (eds.), *Handbook of Qualitative Research.* Thousand Oaks, Calif.: Sage, 1994.

Sutcliffe, K. "Organizational Environments and Organizational Information Processing." In F. M. Jablin, and L. L. Putnam (eds.), *The New Handbook of Organizational Communication.* Thousand Oaks, Calif.: Sage, 2001.

Weick, K. E. *Sensemaking in Organizations.* Thousand Oaks, Calif.: Sage, 1995.

Weick, K. E. *Making Sense of the Organization.* Malden, Mass.: Blackwell, 2001.

Yngvesson, B. "Responses to Grievance Behavior: Extended Cases in a Fishing Community." *American Ethnologist,* 1976, *3,* 353–373.

Yngvesson, B. "The Atlantic Fisherman." In L. Nader, and H. F. Todd, Jr., (eds.), *The Disputing Process: Law in Ten Societies.* New York: Columbia University Press, 1978.

Yngvesson, B. "Making Law at the Doorway: The Clerk, the Court, and the Construction of Community Order in a New England Town." *Law & Society Review,* 1988, *22,* 409–449.

Yngvesson, B. *Virtuous Citizens, Disruptive Subjects: Order and Complaint in a New England Court.* New York: Routledge, 1993.

Iwona L. Kusztal is an assistant professor in the Department of Communication at La Salle University in Philadelphia. Her work focuses on conflict processes in organizations—particularly the role of discourse in conflict emergence and transformation.

Kestner, P. B., and Ray, L. *The Conflict Resolution Training Program: Leader's Manual.* San Francisco: Jossey-Bass, 2002.

REVIEWED BY MELINDA OSTERMEYER

Prudence Bowman Kestner and Larry Ray consolidated their fifty years of cumulative experience teaching people about communication, negotiation, and alternative dispute resolution (ADR) into this easy-to-use instruction guide. The authors set forth the underlying principle that "training methods and information suggest that almost anyone can learn, intellectually and experientially, successful ways to deal with themselves and others and to find common ground" (p. xi). To this end, Kestner and Ray provide readers with a step-by-step approach for delivering training programs related to conflict and conflict management, communication, values, perspectives, power, creativity, consensus, negotiation, mediation, and arbitration. In addition, they provide a compilation of related exercises—annotated with helpful trainer tips—and nineteen scenarios for use during simulated role-plays. (The accompanying publication, Kestner, P. B., and Ray, L. *The Conflict Resolution Training Program: Participant's Manual,* San Francisco: Jossey-Bass, 2002, includes only the exercises and role-play scenarios for use by participants during an actual training program.)

The *Leader's Manual* is particularly useful to individuals less versed in skill-based training for adults, as well as being useful to those new to the fields of conflict management and ADR. The first chapter provides basic information about the design and delivery of any and all training programs, and the information provided is practical and simple enough to readily use. It covers the most mundane details, such as a list of recommended refreshments to serve in the morning and throughout the training day, as well as several schematics showing various ways tables and chairs might be arranged to accommodate large and small groups of participants.

It also provides a conceptual framework, outlining factors to consider when designing conflict management or ADR training programs. The authors stress the importance of articulating the purpose of the training, which for most of the training ideas presented is "to give trainees a clearer understanding of conflict-resolving communication, negotiation and/or mediation processes, the stages of each, and the skills appropriate to each stage" (p. 6). They highlight selecting appropriate training methodologies, such as lectures, worksheets, and experiential exercises, and sequencing these activities to aid learning and to accomplish training objectives. By way of example of these and other training presets, Kestner and Ray offer a sample training plan designed to help readers create their own training agendas and implement the lessons described in the book.

Subsequent chapters of the book are devoted to specific aspects of conflict management, communication, and ADR processes. By way of a brief introduction to the topic, each chapter provides abbreviated substantive information that can be presented to training participants by the trainer as a general overview. While helpful for those less familiar with this subject matter, the information provided will likely be considered simplistic to those with conflict management experience. Nevertheless, it provides a good summary of the basic concepts.

That being said, the greater value of this manual is the series of worksheets and experiential activities that are offered to illustrate specific teaching points. Together with each activity are *tips* about the time and materials needed, the procedures to follow when executing the activity, and trainer's notes about key points to highlight when facilitating discussions related to the activity. While this manual may be most helpful to those with less experience, even the most seasoned conflict management trainers or academic instructors can benefit from a multitude of training activities and ideas packaged in a single reference book.

The manual is user-friendly in format and content. For example, principles of adult learning and the differences between "feedback" and "criticism" serve as lead-ins to the chapter on the introductory phase of training. The chapter goes on to provide a laundry list of opening remarks and activities, beginning with directing the participants to a table for registration and materials when they first walk into the room and ending with the participants clarifying their expectations of the training and creating group norms for how they will interact with each other during the training. Thereafter, the chapter offers four activities during which training participants introduce themselves to their peers. The activities vary in length and complexity, and they offer different opportunities to highlight diverse discussion points. A sampling of discussions possible as a result of the activities presented includes stereotyping, valuing humor, managing change, and eliciting information without polarizing others.

The chapter on conflict and conflict management provides several worksheets for participants to reflect on their personal reactions and experiences with conflict, their own conflict management styles, and their strategies to adjust the way they approach conflict. Worksheets serve as the primary basis for a large portion of the activities in this manual—worksheets to prompt self-reflection, worksheets to focus the participant's thinking, worksheets to practice how to phrase open questions or formulate "I" statements and so forth, and worksheets that serve as brief "quizzes" on various topics. Participants complete the worksheets and share their results with their training peers in pairs, in small groups, or in the group as a whole. Again, trainer's notes accompany each worksheet so that the discussions facilitated by the trainer link teaching points and build upon the participants' real-life experiences.

In addition to worksheets, the chapters related to specific skills provide a variety of experiential activities. The chapter on conflict-resolution communication focuses on styles of communication, active listening, emphatic responses, questioning, target words, and body language. Likewise, the chapter on values, perspectives, and power highlights how our judgments, stereotypes, and perceptions are often grounded in our values. The chapter on creativity sets up situations during which participants experience thinking in innovative and nonconventional ways as they attempt to solve unique problems.

The chapters devoted to skills complement the chapters that focus to a greater degree on process. The dispute resolution continuum provides an introduction to the chapters on consensus, negotiation, mediation and arbitration. Kestner and Ray discuss what factors make one process work more effectively than another in resolving specific types of disputes, and they take the reader step by step through the stages of each process. A sampling of scenarios gives participants the chance to practice resolving disputes through these different ADR processes during simulation role-plays. The brief case facts provide a simple story line, from which the training participants can build their roles as neighbors, workplace colleagues, landlords or tenants, consumers or merchants, or litigants involved with cases pending in the civil, family, and penal courts.

I first used the *Leader's Manual* in conjunction with a Train-the-Mediation-Trainer program I recently conducted in Zambia. I was training the country's first group of mediation trainers, who would spearhead all subsequent mediator training efforts throughout the country for the next several years. The group had mediated for a few years, but none of them had ever designed or delivered mediation training. Their responsibilities as the country's first group of trainers were significant, and they were simultaneously nervous and excited about the prospects. The *Leader's Manual* served as an excellent foundation for this group; it will be a supplemental reference and source for experiential activities and training ideas as they adapt their first training program and create new training programs in the years to come. Many others will find the manual equally valuable.

Melinda Ostermeyer is a conflict management and organizational consultant.

False Dichotomies and Asking the Right Questions

JOHN WADE

This is a comment on a recent article entitled "Enacting and Reproducing Social and Individual Identity Through Mediation" by Ho-Beng Chia, Chee-Leong Chong, Joo-Eng Lee-Partridge, Chantel Chu Shi Hwee, and Sharon Francesca Koh Wei-Fei, in Conflict Resolution Quarterly, *2000, 19(1).*

The writing of these comments itself raises the following cross-cultural issues: When is it appropriate to debate in public? How can debates take place constructively without loss of face? How can a society or sub-culture manage the tension between complexity and simplicity? I make the following comments in an attempt to be helpful and to erect signposts on certain dangerous paths. The conflict management movement in many countries (including my own) is replete with examples of practitioners and theorists jumping out of a frying pan into a fire.

The article reports how some Chinese-Malaysian village mediators were interviewed about their own mediation behaviors. Their self-reports suggested that these village mediators were respected and evaluative and that they emphasized community values, recommended solutions (thereby saving face for the disputants), were well known by the disputants, and encouraged social harmony. The article notes that this apparent Chinese-Malaysian village mediator behavior was different from the behaviors suggested in a certain facilitative "model" taught by foreign trainers who had visited Malaysia and Singapore.

In itself, such a study of self-perceived village mediator behavior, emphasizing that reported behavior does not match a particular model of mediation, is commonplace and potentially helpful. However, in my opinion, the article is filled with silences and errors that are also common and potentially instructive. Each of the following comments emphasizes that asking the right question is half the answer. The silences and errors include the following.

Catalogue of mediation models. No mention is made of the possibility or likelihood that many models of mediation are operating in Malaysia. The "village" model extracted from these few interviews is not labeled as one among many.

The article attacks a paper tiger when it stereotypes an inflexible, rule-bound model of facilitative mediation that allegedly

- Is not interested in relationships or third parties
- Avoids being judgmental
- Does not need respect or moral authority for the mediator
- Has no ties to either party
- Avoids proposing any solutions
- Is not interested in tradition
- Does not use notions of forgiveness or "let bygones be bygones"

It is doubtful that such a rule-bound paper tiger model of mediation exists in practice or theory anywhere.

Discovery of actual mediator behavior. One clear lesson in the mediation movement is to not rely on mediators who self-report on what we do. Yet the article makes the double error of relying on what visiting teachers allegedly *said* is done five thousand miles away and what traditional village mediators *say* they do nearby.

The next important question concerns how to discover the diversity of what mediators do, beyond myths, propaganda, and self-report.

Marketing competing mediation models. The article sets up a competitive tone of "them" versus "us." This is a worldwide pattern with new competitive products, including various mediation models. "Here is model X, which is unsuitable for . . . and contrasting model Y, which is suitable for. . . ."

Expressing this doubt about the suitability of any service or product is admirable and is an essential attitude for any responsible service provider. However, if the doubt leads to the unquestioning embrace of my service instead of yours, then we have jumped out of the frying pan into the fire—physiotherapy instead of surgery, exercise instead of chemicals, evaluative mediation instead of facilitative mediation, and so forth. The best marketer wins—temporarily.

Diagnosis: Which model for which disputes? The article suggests that the alleged behaviors of village mediators are culturally appropriate in Malaysia. Conversely, it suggests that the model introduced by some visiting teachers is inappropriate for Malaysia. Both of these are conclusions. What is the question? The standard question in all countries is, What model of mediation is appropriate for which kind of disputes with which kind of disputants?

Once again, the right question is half the answer.

Would the five authors personally use an evaluative village mediator for their own international, national, personal, and business disputes? If not, why not?

By missing the right diagnostic question, the article is in danger of perpetuating premature positional bargaining over the most "culturally sensitive" model. In the writer's experience, this leads to an unnecessarily hostile debate between the many subcultures within each country. "The basic model should reflect my culture, not yours," "You are disrespectful to my culture by suggesting that," "You are a dinosaur to make those cultural generalizations about our multi-cultural society," and so forth.

The failure to ask the right diagnostic question has, in Australia, the United Kingdom, and the United States, led to vitriolic competition between counselors and mediators, litigators and mediators, and evaluative, facilitative, and transformative mediators. I am hoping that Malaysia may be able to avoid some of our mistakes.

Diagnosis: How should a model be adapted to suit the cultural practices of the various disputants? This question is an important offshoot of the previous diagnostic question. The question is whether the "culture" or subculture is unemployed mine workers, upper-class Hong Kong Chinese, articulate Aborigines, or a motorcycle club.

The article most helpfully objects to any mediation model or practice that ignores possible cultural adaptations. However, the article appears to jump to a conclusion by recommending a particular set of cultural adaptations—namely, the alleged behaviors of village mediators. When will the village model be an entirely unsuitable and insensitive starting point for disputes within the geographical boundaries of Malaysia? How can a village model be adapted when there is a variety of different cultural groups at a mediation or negotiation?

What is "success"? The article by implication suggests that the traditional village mediation model is "successful" in Malaysia. Once again, this is a premature conclusion. On what criteria is success being determined? By what methods is each element of success being measured? Comparatively, is this observed and praised service more or less successful than inaction, litigation, personal negotiation, or threatening letters? What do the customers say about "excellence," "competence," or "incompetence" of the (village) mediators?

Any alleged popularity of one conflict management process should also be considered in the context of economics, power, education, and culture before it can be considered a success. For example, evaluative mediation may be more successful, whereas litigation is expensive, distant, and corrupt. Are traditional services more likely to be accepted in certain cultures because criticism and reform are less tolerated? Are successful mediators politically and economically powerful (like the United States in international mediation) so that they have the ability to punish disputants who do not comply with their recommendations?

The article gives one tantalizing hint that the observed and praised methods of village mediators may not always be successful in Malaysia when it suddenly states that "the traditional model of mediation reinforces the status quo by reproducing the past (which may or may not be appropriate for today's environment)" (p. 68).

I hope these comments will be received in the spirit in which they are intended. Knowledge of how new movements, including mediation, have historically been adopted, adapted, or rejected in various cultures may help one avoid some of the mistakes of the past. To repeat, the right question is half the answer.

John Wade is professor and director of the Dispute Resolution Center at Bond University in Queensland, Australia. He practices as a mediator and teaches mediation courses each year in Australia, the United States, the United Kingdom, Indonesia, Hong Kong, and New Zealand.

INFORMATION FOR CONTRIBUTORS

Conflict Resolution Quarterly publishes scholarship on relationships between theory, research, and practice in the conflict management and dispute resolution field to promote more effective professional applications. *Conflict Resolution Quarterly* is sponsored by the Association for Conflict Resolution (formerly the Academy of Family Mediators, the Society for Professionals in Dispute Resolution and the Conflict Resolution Education Network).

Articles may focus on any aspect of the conflict resolution process or context, but a primary focus is the behavior, role, and impact of third parties in effectively handling conflict. All theoretical and methodological orientations are welcome. Submission of scholarship with the following emphases is encouraged:

- Discussion of a variety of third-party conflict resolution practices, including dialogue, facilitation, facilitated negotiation, mediation, fact-finding, and arbitration
- Analyses of disputant and third-party behavior, preference, and reaction to conflict situations and conflict management processes
- Consideration of conflict processes in a variety of conflict contexts, including family, organizational, community, court, health care, commercial, international, and educational contexts
- Sensitivity to relational, social, and cultural contexts that define and impact conflict
- Interdisciplinary analyses of conflict resolution and scholarship providing insights applicable across conflict resolution contexts
- Discussion of conflict resolution training and education processes, program development, and program evaluation and impact for programs focusing on the development of more competent conflict resolution in educational, organizational, community, or professional contexts

A defining focus of the journal is the relationships among theory, research, and practice. All articles should specifically address the implications of theory for practice and research directions, how research can better inform practice, or how research can contribute to theory development with important implications for practice.

Conflict Resolution Quarterly publishes conventional articles and other features, including the following:

- *State-of-the-art articles:* Articles providing a comprehensive reporting of current literature on a specific topic and a critique of that theory and research in terms of how well it informs conflict practice.

- *Implications-for-practice commentary:* Readers' comments on the implications for practice of previously published articles, discussing how the articles have informed them in terms of practice.

- *Book reviews:* Reviews of current books on conflict management and dispute resolution. Preference is given to book review essays that review three or more books in a related topic area in light of current scholarship in that area.

- *Training and education notes:* Short articles focusing on the practice of dispute resolution training, studies of dispute resolution training, or reviews of curricula or software programs for dispute resolution training.

Manuscript Preparation

All submissions should be prepared according to the *Chicago Manual of Style* (14th edition, University of Chicago Press). Double-space everything in the manuscript, including quotes and references. Indent the first line of each paragraph and leave no extra space between paragraphs. Margins should be at least one inch wide, and there should be no more than 250 words per manuscript page. Use 8½-inch × 11-inch nonerasable bond paper and type or print on one side only. The printed copy from word processors must be in regular typewriter face, not dot matrix type.

The text should be directed to a multidisciplinary audience and be as readable and practical as possible. Illustrate theoretical ideas with specific examples, explain technical terms in nontechnical language, and keep the style clear. Do not include graphs or statistical tables unless necessary for clarity. Spell out such abbreviations as *e.g., etc., i.e., et al.,* and *vs.* in their English equivalents—in other words, use *for example, and so on, that is, and others,* and *versus* (except in legal cases, where *v.* is used).

Conventional Articles and State-of-the-Art Articles. These papers should be no longer than thirty double-spaced pages of text (or 7,500 words). Submissions should include a cover page providing title and author name(s) and contact information (address, telephone number, and e-mail address). Submissions should also include a short abstract of the article (no more than 100 words). Hard-copy paper submissions should include three copies of the paper with a detachable cover page.

Practitioner Responses, Implications-for-Practice Commentary, Book Reviews, and Training and Education Notes. These features should be no more than ten double-spaced pages of text (or 2,500 words). Submissions should contain a cover page clearly indicating the nature of the submission and providing author name(s) and contact information. Papers can be submitted via e-mail if sent as a file attachment prepared in Word 6.0 or 7.0 or in rich text format. Hard-copy paper submissions should include three copies of the paper with a detachable cover page.

Citations and References. Cite all sources of quotations or attributed ideas in the text, including the original page number of each direct quotation and statistic, according to the following examples:

Knight (1983) argues cogently that references are a pain in the neck. As one authority states, "References are a pain in the neck" (Knight, 1983, p. 35).

Do not use footnotes. Incorporate all footnote material into the text proper, perhaps within parentheses. (Brief *endnotes,* if used sparingly, are acceptable and should be double-spaced in numerical order and placed before the reference section. Endnotes must not contain bibliographical data).

Use the following examples in typing references:

Single-author book or pamphlet
Hunter, J. E. *Meta-Analysis: Cumulating Research Findings Across Studies.* Newbury Park, Calif.: Sage, 1982.

Multiple-author book or pamphlet
Hammond, D. C., Hepworth, D. H., and Smith, V. G. *Improving Therapeutic Communication: A Guide for Developing Effective Techniques.* San Francisco: Jossey-Bass, 1977.

Edited book/multiple edition
Brakel, S. J., and Rock, R. S. (eds.). *The Mentally Disabled and the Law.* (2nd ed.) Chicago: University of Chicago Press, 1971.

Chapter in an edited book

Patterson, G. R. "Beyond Technology: The Next Stage in the Development of Parent Training." In L. L'Abate (ed.), *Handbook of Family Psychology and Therapy*. Vol. 2. Homewood, Ill.: Dorsey Press, 1985.

Journal or magazine article

Aussieker, B., and Garabino, J. W. "Measuring Faculty Unionism: Quantity and Quality." *Industrial Relations,* 1973, *12*(1), 117–124.

Paper read at a meeting

Sherman, L. W., Gartin, P. R., Doi, D., and Miler, S. "The Effects of Jail Time on Drunk Drivers." Paper presented at the American Society of Criminology, Atlanta, Nov. 6, 1986.

Unpublished report

Keim, S. T., and Carney, M. K. "A Cost-Benefit Study of Selected Clinical Education Programs for Professional and Allied Health Personnel." Arlington, Va.: Bureau of Business and Economic Research, University of Texas, 1975.

Government report

Florida Advisory Council on Intergovernmental Relations. *Impact Fees in Florida.* Tallahassee: Florida Advisory Council on Intergovernmental Relations, 1986.

Unpublished dissertation

Johnson, W. P. "A Study of the Acceptance of Management Performance Evaluation Recommendations by Federal Agencies: Lessons from GAO Reports Issued in FY 1983." Unpublished doctoral dissertation, Department of Business Administration, George Mason University, Washington, D.C., 1986.

Figures, Tables, and Exhibits. Clean copies of figures should accompany the manuscript. Upon an article's acceptance, authors must provide camera-ready artwork. Tables, figures, and exhibits should be double-spaced on separate pages, and table notes should be keyed to the body of the table with letters rather than with numbers or asterisks. Exhibits (used in place of appendixes) should also be typed double-spaced on separate pages. All figures, tables, and exhibits should have short, descriptive titles and must be called out in the text.

Publication Process

When a manuscript is accepted for publication, authors are asked to sign a letter of agreement granting the publisher the right to copyedit, publish, and copyright the material. Manuscripts under review for possible publication in *Conflict Resolution Quarterly* should not be submitted for review elsewhere or have been previously published elsewhere.

Article submissions and questions regarding editorial matters should be sent to:

Tricia S. Jones, Editor
Conflict Resolution Quarterly
Department of Psychological Studies
College of Education
Temple University
Philadelphia, PA 19122
tsjones@astro.temple.edu

ORDERING INFORMATION

MAIL ORDERS TO:
Jossey-Bass
989 Market Street
San Francisco, CA 94103-1741

PHONE subscription or single-copy orders toll free to (888) 378-2537 or to (415) 433-1767 (toll call).

FAX orders toll free to (888) 481-2665.

SUBSCRIPTIONS cost $75.00 for individuals in the United States, Canada, and Mexico; $175.00 for institutions, agencies, and libraries in the United States; $215.00 for institutions, agencies, and libraries in Canada and Mexico; and $99.00 for individuals and $249.00 for institutions, agencies, and libraries in the rest of the world. Standing orders are accepted. New York residents, add local sales tax. (For subscriptions outside the United States, orders must be prepaid in U.S. dollars by check drawn on a U.S. bank or charged to VISA, MasterCard, or American Express.)

SINGLE COPIES cost $36.00 plus shipping (see below) when payment accompanies order. California, New Jersey, New York, and Washington, D.C. residents, please include appropriate sales tax. Canadian residents, add GST and any local taxes. Billed orders will be charged shipping and handling. No billed shipments to Post Office boxes. (Orders from outside the United States must be prepaid in U.S. dollars by check drawn on a U.S. bank or charged to VISA, MasterCard, or American Express.)

SHIPPING (single copies only): $5.00 for first item, $3.00 for each additional item. Call for information on overnight delivery or shipments outside the United States.

ALL ORDERS must include either the name of an individual or an official purchase order number. Please submit your orders as follows:
Subscriptions: specify issue (for example, CRQ19:1) with which you would like subscription to begin.
Single copies: specify volume and issue number.

MICROFILM available from University Microfilms, 300 North Zeeb Road, Ann Arbor, MI 48106.

DISCOUNTS FOR QUANTITY ORDERS are available. For information, please write to Jossey-Bass, 989 Market Street, San Francisco, CA 94103-1741.

LIBRARIANS are encouraged to write to Jossey-Bass for a free sample issue.

VISIT THE JOSSEY-BASS HOME PAGE at http://www.josseybass.com on the World Wide Web for an order form or information about other titles of interest.

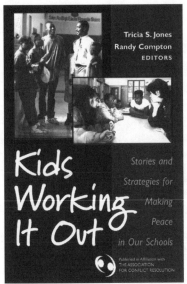